Science

Grade 8

ISBN 978-0-544-26818-0

1 2 3 4 5 6 7 8 9 10   XXXX   22 21 20 19 18 17 16 15 14 13

4500000000   B C D E F G

Core Skills Science
GRADE 8
Table of Contents

Introduction

The *Core Skills Science* series offers parents and educators high-quality, curriculum-based products that align with the Next Generation Science Standards* Disciplinary Core Ideas for grades 1–8. The *Core Skills Science* series provides informative and grade-appropriate readings on a wide variety of topics in life, earth, and physical science. Two pages of worksheets follow each reading passage. The book includes:

- clear illustrations, making scientific concepts accessible to young learners

- engaging reading passages, covering a wide variety of topics in life, earth, and physical science

- logically sequenced activities, transitioning smoothly from basic comprehension to higher-order thinking skills

- comprehension questions, ascertaining that students understand what they have read

- vocabulary activities, challenging students to show their understanding of scientific terms

- critical thinking activities, increasing students' ability to analyze, synthesize, and evaluate scientific information

- questions in standardized-test format, helping prepare students for state exams

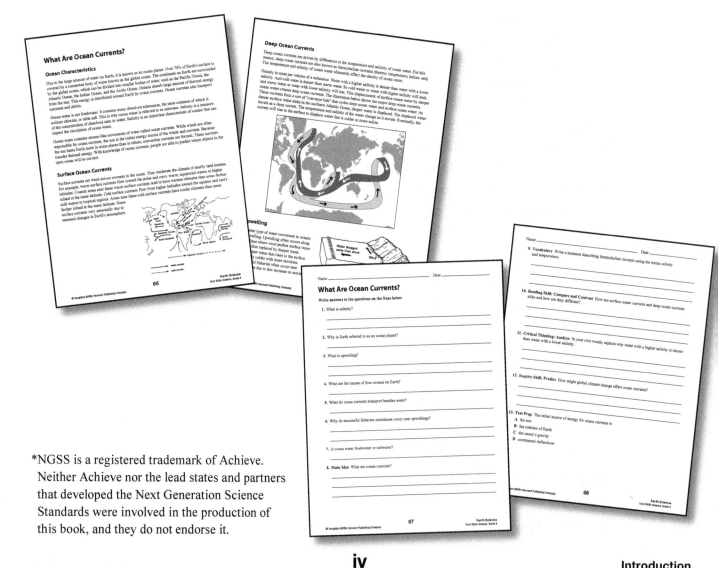

*NGSS is a registered trademark of Achieve. Neither Achieve nor the lead states and partners that developed the Next Generation Science Standards were involved in the production of this book, and they do not endorse it.

How Do Animals Reproduce?

Kingdom Animalia

Animals are part of kingdom Animalia. Animals are multicellular organisms with cells that lack the rigid cell wall that plant cells have. Animals are heterotrophs, which means they cannot produce their own food like autotrophs. Animals must rely on eating autotrophs or other heterotrophs to obtain nutrition. Members of kingdom Animalia are very diverse. Examples include earthworms, insects, snails, reptiles, birds, and mammals.

Animals can reproduce through sexual reproduction or asexual reproduction. Asexual reproduction requires only one parent and results in offspring with genotypes that are exact copies of their parent's genotype. Sexual reproduction requires two parents and produces offspring that share traits with their parents but are not exactly like either parent. The majority of animals reproduce through sexual reproduction, though there are some animal species that are capable of asexual reproduction. Figure A below is an example of sexual reproduction and Figure B is an example of asexual reproduction.

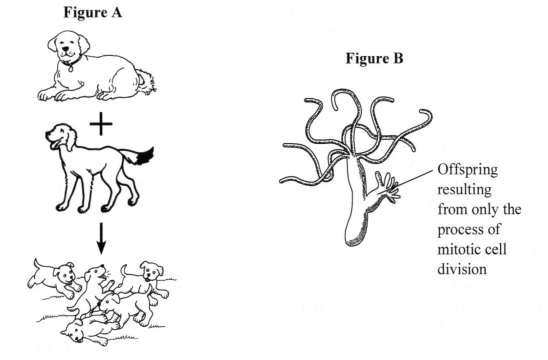

Figure A

Figure B

Offspring resulting from only the process of mitotic cell division

Sexual Reproduction

In sexual reproduction, organisms reproduce by joining sex cells, or gametes, to form the first cell of a new individual. The gametes are haploid; that is, they contain one set of unpaired chromosomes. Sexual reproduction requires two parents. Through meiosis, each parent forms reproductive cells that have one-half the number of chromosomes of regular body cells, or somatic cells. In this manner, a diploid mother and father give rise to haploid gametes. These gametes join during fertilization to form diploid offspring. Because both parents contribute genetic material, the offspring have traits of both parents but are not exactly like either parent. Sexual reproduction involving haploid gametes occurs in eukaryotic organisms, including humans. Sexual reproduction is a source of genetic diversity in a population.

1

Life Science
Core Skills Science, Grade 8

Meiosis

Consider the common fruit fly, which has four pairs of chromosomes. One set of chromosomes came from one "parent," and the other set came from a second parent. We say that the two sets of chromosomes are homologous and that the cell is diploid. Diploid cells contain two complete sets of chromosomes, and thus two complete sets of genes. The gametes of the fruit fly, however, are haploid. How can the diploid cells of the fruit fly produce gametes with only half their number of chromosomes? The answer is meiosis. Meiosis is a form of cell division that halves the number of chromosomes when forming specialized reproductive cells, such as gametes or spores. Meiosis involves two divisions of the nucleus—meiosis I and meiosis II. Before meiosis begins, the DNA in the original cell is replicated. Thus, meiosis starts with homologous chromosomes. Homologous chromosomes are similar in size, shape, and genetic content.

Asexual Reproduction

In asexual reproduction, only one parent cell is needed. The structures inside the cell are copied, and then the parent cell divides, making two exact copies. This type of cell reproduction is known as mitosis. Most of the cells in your body and most single-celled organisms reproduce in this way. An individual produced by asexual reproduction is a clone, an organism that is genetically identical to its parent. Asexual reproduction does not increase the genetic diversity in a population. However, asexual reproduction does have the advantage of allowing isolated organisms to reproduce without finding a mate.

Many invertebrates reproduce through asexual reproductive processes such as fission, budding, or fragmentation followed by regeneration. During fission, a parent organism duplicates its genetic material and then divides into two separate organisms of the same size. Budding occurs when smaller, genetically identical offspring split, or bud, from the parent organism. Some multicellular eukaryotes undergo fragmentation, a type of reproduction in which the body breaks into several pieces. Some or all of these fragments later develop into complete adults when missing parts are regrown. Fragmentation and regeneration is similar to vegetative propagation, in which pieces from a plant grow into a new plant.

Human Reproduction

Humans reproduce through sexual reproduction. Human body cells have 46 chromosomes, or 23 pairs of chromosomes. But human sex cells are different. They have 23 chromosomes—half the usual number. These sex cells are made during meiosis. For example, the female sex cell, or egg cell, has 23 chromosomes, and the male sex cell, or sperm cell, also has 23 chromosomes. The new cell that forms when an egg cell is fertilized by a sperm cell has 46 chromosomes.

Sexual reproduction provides a powerful means of quickly making different combinations of genes among individuals. Such genetic diversity is the raw material for evolution. In humans, for example, each gamete receives one chromosome from each of 23 pairs of homologous chromosomes. Which of the two chromosomes that an offspring receives from each of the 23 pairs is a matter of chance. This random distribution of homologous chromosomes during meiosis is called independent assortment. Each of the 23 pairs of chromosomes segregates (separates) independently. Thus, 2^{23} (about 8 million) gametes with different gene combinations can be produced from one original cell by this mechanism. Crossing-over adds even more recombination of genetic material.

How Do Animals Reproduce?

Write answers to the questions on the lines below.

1. Tigers reproduce by sexual reproduction. How many parents are needed to produce a baby tiger?

   _____

2. Name two characteristics of animals.

   _____

3. How many pairs of chromosomes does a human body cell have?

   _____

4. What is one advantage of sexual reproduction?

   _____

5. What is one advantage of asexual reproduction?

   _____

6. What is budding?

   _____

7. Which type of reproduction do the majority of animals use?

   _____

8. **Main Idea** How do animals reproduce?

   _____
   _____
   _____
   _____
   _____
   _____

Overview of Meiosis

Life Science
Core Skills Science, Grade 8

9. **Vocabulary** Write a sentence using the terms *meiosis* and *sexual reproduction*.

_____

_____

_____

10. **Reading Skill: Main Idea and Details** How many chromosomes occur in the new cell formed when human male and female sex cells carrying genetic information unite?

_____

_____

11. **Critical Thinking: Evaluate** What would happen if diploid organisms reproduced by sexual reproduction without first producing sex cells through meiosis?

_____

_____

_____

12. **Inquiry Skill: Use Models** Draw a diagram that models sexual and asexual reproduction in an organism that has four pairs of chromosomes, or eight total chromosomes. Include the number of chromosomes for parent and offspring organisms, and intermediate sex cells in your model of sexual reproduction.

13. **Test Prep** Which of the following statements about asexual reproduction is NOT true?

    A Only one parent sex cell is needed.

    B The offspring are copies of the parent.

    C Most single-celled organisms reproduce this way.

    D It results in more variation in species than does sexual reproduction.

What Is Cellular Respiration?

Energy

All living things use energy to grow, to move, and to process information. Without energy, life soon stops. Living organisms carry out many different chemical reactions in order to obtain and then use energy to run the processes of life. Metabolism is the sum of all of the chemical reactions carried out in an organism.

The process of eating and digesting food involves extracting energy from that food. As the food is digested, chemical reactions convert the chemical energy in food molecules to forms of energy that can be used within the body's cells. This process is called cellular respiration.

When a log burns, the energy stored in wood is released quickly as heat and light. But in cells, the chemical energy stored in food molecules is released gradually in a series of enzyme-assisted chemical reactions. The product of one chemical reaction becomes a reactant in the next reaction. In the breakdown of starch, for example, each reaction releases energy.

Cellular Respiration

Cellular respiration is the process cells use to harvest the energy in organic compounds, particularly glucose. Cellular respiration uses sugar and oxygen gas as the reactants to produce energy, water, and carbon dioxide. The breakdown of glucose during cellular respiration is expressed in this equation:

$$\underset{\text{glucose}}{C_6H_{12}O_6} + \underset{\substack{\text{oxygen}\\\text{gas}}}{6O_2} \xrightarrow{\text{enzymes}} \underset{\substack{\text{carbon}\\\text{dioxide}}}{6CO_2} + \underset{\text{water}}{6H_2O} + \underset{\text{ATP}}{\text{energy}}$$

Cellular respiration occurs in two stages. Stage 1: Glucose is converted to pyruvate, producing a small amount of adenosine triphosphate (ATP) and the enzyme NADH.

Stage 2: When oxygen is present, pyruvate and NADH are used to make a large amount of ATP. This process is called aerobic respiration. Aerobic respiration occurs in the mitochondria of eukaryotic cells (cells with a nucleus) and in the cell membrane of prokaryotic cells (cells without a nucleus). When oxygen is not present, pyruvate is converted to either lactate or ethanol and carbon dioxide through anaerobic processes called fermentation. Any metabolic process that requires oxygen is an aerobic process. Metabolic processes that do not require oxygen are called anaerobic, meaning "without air."

ATP

When cells break down food molecules, some of the energy in the molecules is released as heat. Much of the remaining energy is stored temporarily in molecules of ATP, or adenosine triphosphate. ATP is composed of a single adenine ring, a ribose sugar, and three energy-storing phosphate groups. Like money, ATP is a portable form of energy "currency" inside cells.

ATP delivers energy wherever that energy is needed in a cell. Cells break down ATP to release the energy it stores. The energy released when ATP is broken down can be used to power other chemical reactions, such as those that build molecules. In cells, most chemical reactions require less energy than is released from the breakdown of ATP. Therefore, enough energy is released from ATP to drive most of a cell's activities.

As in most organisms, cells in the human body transfer the energy in organic compounds, especially glucose, to ATP through a process called cellular respiration. When a person breathes in oxygen, the production of ATP is more efficient, although some ATP is made without oxygen.

Cellular Respiration and Photosynthesis

Photosynthesis is the process by which plants and some microorganisms use sunlight, carbon dioxide, and water to produce sugar and oxygen. The sugar molecules produced during photosynthesis are either used immediately for energy needs or stored for future use. An example of storing energy for future use is a plant storing energy in its roots or tubers. The plant can use the energy later, or an animal can eat the plant and its roots and use the nutrition for its own energy needs. For example, some single-cell organisms called paramecia eat other single-cell organisms called bacteria. Many animals eat plants. Humans eat plants or animals that have eaten plants. Energy flows from the sun to plants, from these plants to plant-eating organisms, and from plant-eating organisms to meat-eating organisms.

Food, in the form of sugar, is produced during photosynthesis, and the food is broken down during cellular respiration. Photosynthesis and cellular respiration are two related processes that cycle energy and matter throughout ecosystems.

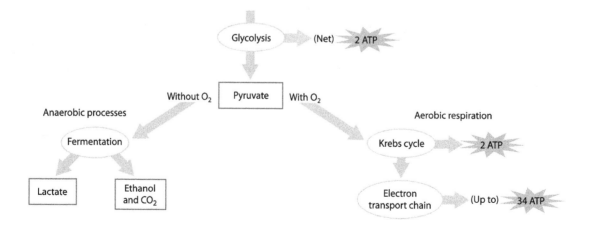

What Is Cellular Respiration?

Fill in the blank.

1. Plants and animals carry out _____ to break down food into energy.

2. The _____ of cellular respiration are sugar and oxygen.

3. The products of cellular respiration are _____, _____,

   and _____.

4. _____ is the sum of all chemical reactions carried out in an organism.

5. Cells use _____ as an energy currency to complete reactions within the cell.

6. A(n) _____ process does not require oxygen.

7. Cellular respiration is one way that _____ and _____
   are cycled through an ecosystem.

8. **Main Idea** What is cellular respiration?

   _____

   _____

   _____

   _____

   _____

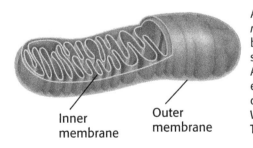

Inner membrane   Outer membrane

A **mitochondrion** (plural, *mitochondria*) is an organelle that breaks down organic compounds, such as sugars, to make ATP. ATP is a molecule that stores energy in its chemical bonds and carries energy to where the cell needs it. When bonds in ATP break, energy is released. The cell uses this energy for its life process.

7

9. **Vocabulary** Use the terms *cellular respiration*, *photosynthesis*, and *ATP* in a paragraph that describes the origination of energy used by animals.

_____

_____

_____

_____

10. **Reading Skill: Main Idea and Details** What parts make up an ATP molecule?

_____

_____

11. **Critical Thinking: Synthesize** Bacteria do not have a nucleus. Why does cellular respiration in bacteria take place in cell membranes instead of in mitochondria?

_____

_____

_____

12. **Inquiry Skill: Using Models** Draw a diagram that models the relationship between photosynthesis and cellular respiration.

13. **Test Prep** Which of the following pairings shows the substance released during cellular respiration and the cellular structure that is responsible for that process?

A O_2 and chloroplast

B ATP and chloroplast

C CO_2 and mitochondria

D glucose and mitochondria

How Are Populations Modeled?

Components of an Ecosystem

An organism's environment consists of all the things that affect an organism. These things can be divided into two groups. All of the organisms that live together and interact with one another make up the biotic part of the environment. The abiotic part of the environment consists of the nonliving factors, such as water, soil, light, and temperature. The environment can also be organized into different levels. The first level is made up of an individual organism.

The second level is larger and is made of individuals of a species that live together in one place at the same time, which form a population. For example, a salt marsh is a coastal area where grass-like plants grow and is home to many animals. Each animal is a part of a population, or a group of individuals of the same species that live together. For example, all of the seaside sparrows that live in the same salt marsh are members of a population. The individuals in the population often compete with one another for food, nesting space, and mates.

A community (the third level) consists of all the populations of species that live and interact in an area. All the animals and plants in the salt marsh form a salt-marsh community. The populations in a community depend on one another for food, shelter, and many other things.

An ecosystem (the fourth level) is made up of a community of organisms and the abiotic environment of the community. An ecologist studying the ecosystem could examine how organisms interact, as well as how temperature, precipitation, and soil characteristics affect the organisms. For example, the rivers that empty into the salt marsh carry nutrients, such as nitrogen, from the land. These nutrients affect the growth of the cordgrass and algae.

The fifth and final level contains all ecosystems, which form the biosphere. The biosphere is the part of Earth where life exists. It extends from the deepest parts of the ocean to high in the air where plant spores drift. Ecologists study the biosphere to learn how organisms interact with the abiotic environment—Earth's atmosphere, water, soil, and rock.

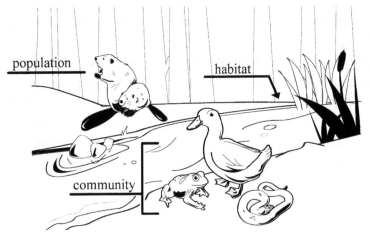

Carrying Capacity

The largest population that an environment can support is known as the carrying capacity. When a population grows larger than its carrying capacity, limiting factors in the environment cause individuals to die off or leave. As individuals die or leave, the population decreases and returns to a size that the environment can support. Sometimes the abiotic factors and limited resources can cause every member of the population to die. The population then becomes extinct.

Population Models

When scientists predict how a population will change, they make a model of the population. The model attempts to exhibit the key characteristics of a real population. By making a change in the model and observing the outcome, scientists can predict what might occur in a real population. A simple population model describes the rate of population growth as the difference between the birthrate and the death rate.

$$r \text{ (rate of growth)} = \text{birthrate} - \text{death rate}$$

Exponential population growth occurs when the rate of population growth stays the same, and as a result, the population size increases steadily. When population size is plotted against time on a graph, the population growth curve resembles a J-shaped curve and is called an exponential growth curve. The rate of growth (r) is multiplied by the current number of individuals in the population (N) in order to determine the number of individuals that will be added to a population.

$$\triangle N \text{(change in population)} = rN$$

However, populations do not usually grow unchecked. Their growth is limited by factors such as predators, disease, and the availability of resources. These factors are called limiting factors. Eventually in an ecosystem, growth slows, and the population may stabilize at the carrying capacity. The population then remains at a steady level.

As a population grows, limited resources eventually become depleted. When this happens, the growth of the population slows. The population model can be adjusted to account for the effect of limited resources, such as food and water. These resources are called density-dependent factors because the rate at which they become depleted depends upon the density of the population that uses them.

The population model that takes into account the declining resources available to populations is called the logistic model of population growth, after the mathematical form of the equation. In this model, exponential growth is limited by a density-dependent factor. Unlike the simple model, the logistic model assumes that birth and death rates vary with population size. When a population is below carrying capacity (K), the growth rate is rapid. However, as the population approaches the carrying capacity, death rates begin to rise and birthrates begin to decline. Competition for food, shelter, mates, and limited resources tends to increase as a population approaches its carrying capacity. The accumulation of wastes also increases. As a result, the rate of growth slows. The population eventually stops growing when birthrate equals the death rate.

$$\triangle N = \frac{rN(K-N)}{K}$$

In real situations, the population may for a short time actually exceed the carrying capacity of its environment. If this happens, deaths will increase and outnumber births until the population falls to the carrying capacity.

© Houghton Mifflin Harcourt Publishing Company

How Are Populations Modeled?

Match each term to its correct definition.

Definitions

_____ 1. rate of growth equals birthrate minus death rate

_____ 2. exponential growth is limited by density-dependent factor

_____ 3. nonliving factors in the environment

_____ 4. largest population that an ecosystem can support

_____ 5. community of organisms and the nonliving environment

_____ 6. population growth stays the same and population size increases steadily

_____ 7. individuals of a species that live together at the same time

_____ 8. part of Earth where life exists

Terms

a. exponential growth model

b. carrying capacity

c. biosphere

d. logistic growth model

e. population

f. abiotic factor

g. simple growth model

h. ecosystem

9. **Main Idea** Why do scientists model populations?

_____

_____

_____

_____

_____

_____

_____

11

10. Vocabulary Explain the difference between the *simple, exponential,* and *logistic growth models.*

_____

_____

_____

_____

11. Reading Skill: Sequence Correctly sequence the hierarchy of an ecosystem from individual to biosphere.

_____

_____

12. Critical Thinking: Analyze How are birthrate and death rate related to the rate of population growth in an ecosystem? Include an equation in your answer.

_____

_____

_____

13. Inquiry Skill: Predict Three species of finches are in competition for the limited resources of an ecosystem. One species prefers fruit to seeds. The second species prefers seeds to fruit. The third species will eat fruit or seeds with equal preference. If the third species is removed from the area, explain how the ecosystem will change.

_____

_____

_____

14. Test Prep Your class has been observing the population growth of a species of Paramecium, a single-celled organism, for 18 days. Your data are shown in the graph below. Food was occasionally added to the test tube in which the paramecia were grown.

What is the carrying capacity of the test-tube environment as long as food is added?

A about 10 paramecia

B about 45 paramecia

C about 90 paramecia

D about 100 paramecia

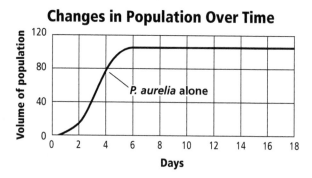

Changes in Population Over Time

12

Life Science
Core Skills Science, Grade 8

How Do Ecosystems Change?

Ecosystems Are Dynamic

An ecosystem, or ecological system, consists of a community and all the physical aspects of its habitat, such as the soil, water, and weather. Earth's ecosystems may seem stable, but they are not static. They change seasonally, they can change suddenly, and they can even change over time. Climate change is one way that ecosystems can change. They can also change through a regular, progressive process called succession.

Succession is the gradual development of a community over time, such as the regrowth of burned areas of Yellowstone National Park. Succession takes place in all communities, not just those affected by disturbances such as forest fires. As succession progresses, older inhabitants die out and new organisms gradually move in. Why does this change take place? One reason is that organisms change their environment, usually a little at a time. As the environment changes, so do the populations living there.

When a volcano forms a new island, a glacier recedes and exposes bare rock, or a fire burns all of the vegetation in an area, a new habitat is created. This change sets off a process of colonization and ecosystem development. The first organisms to live in a new habitat are called pioneer species. The pioneer species where soil is present tend to be small, fast-growing plants. They may make the ground more hospitable for other species. Later waves of plant immigrants may then outcompete and replace the pioneer species.

Primary Succession

Sometimes, a small community starts to grow in an area where other organisms have not previously lived. There is no soil in this area. And usually, there is just bare rock. Over a very long time, a series of organisms live and die on the rock. The rock is slowly transformed into soil. This process is called primary succession. Pioneer species must be able to live in areas with no soil. Lichens and some mosses are typical pioneer species. They physically and chemically break down rocks and help begin the process of soil formation. As lichens and mosses die and decay, the nutrients in their remains enrich the newly forming soil.

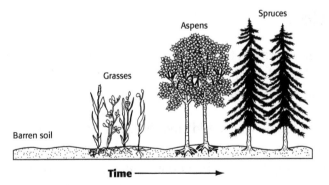

After a number of years, the area becomes able to support small flowering plants, small shrubs, and some grasses. These organisms further the process of soil formation and provide shelter for small animals. The community of living things in the area continues to become more diverse. Eventually, the area becomes able to support trees, other large plants, and larger animals. This process takes many years.

Secondary Succession

Secondary succession, the more common type of succession, occurs where there has been previous growth. Secondary succession occurs in ecosystems that have been disturbed or disrupted by humans, animals, or natural processes such as storms, floods, and earthquakes. Forest fires can also cause secondary succession. Secondary succession can also happen when previously cultivated farmland is abandoned. In these ecosystems, the soil has not been destroyed.

Primary succession and secondary succession have some similarities and some differences. Both are a series of changes that occur after a disturbance in an ecosystem. In both types of succession, ecosystems move toward greater diversity and stability. Primary succession occurs only in areas with no soil and no life, such as newly formed volcanic islands. Secondary succession occurs after a disturbance, such as a forest fire, that leaves the soil intact. As you might expect, secondary succession usually proceeds more quickly than primary succession.

Climax Community

In the early stages of succession, only a few species grow in an area. These species grow quickly and make many seeds that scatter easily. But all species are vulnerable to disease, disturbances, and competition. As a community matures, it may be dominated by well-adapted, slow-growing climax species. Furthermore, as succession proceeds, more species may become established. Keep in mind that a mature community may not always be a forest. A mature community simply has organisms that are well adapted to live together in the same area over time. For example, the plants of the Sonoran Desert are well adapted to the desert's conditions.

Ecological succession is a gradual process of change and replacement of some or all of the species in a community. The process may take hundreds or thousands of years. Scientists once thought that the stages of succession were predictable and that succession always led to the same final community of organisms within any particular ecosystem. Ecologists now recognize that initial conditions and chance play roles in the process of succession. For example, if two species are in competition, a sudden change in the climate may favor the success of one species over the other. For this reason, no two successions are alike.

Example of Succession

The 1980 eruption at Mount St. Helens in the state of Washington has provided an excellent example of succession. This eruption has been described as one of the worst volcanic disasters because more than 44,460 acres of forest were burned and flattened by the force of hot ash and other volcanic debris.

If you visited Mount St. Helens today, you would find that plants and flowers have covered most of the lava, and new trees and shrubs have started to grow. If these organisms at Mount St. Helens continue to grow, over time they will eventually form a climax community. A climax community is a final and stable community. Even though a climax community continues to change in small ways, this type of community may remain the same through time if it is not disturbed.

Name _____ Date _____

How Do Ecosystems Change?

Fill in the blank.

1. Lichens are an example of a(n) _____ species.

2. A volcanic eruption resulting in bare rock can lead to _____ succession.

3. _____ is the gradual change of a community over time.

4. A(n) _____ is a community of organisms and all of the associated environmental factors.

5. The rate of secondary succession is _____ than the rate of primary succession.

6. _____ succession occurs after the disturbance of an ecosystem that had previous growth.

7. A final and stable community is a(n) _____ community.

8. **Main Idea** What is the main cause of succession, whether it is primary or secondary succession?

_____

_____

_____

9. **Vocabulary** Describe how communities can change over time using the terms *succession* and *climax community*.

_____

_____

_____

10. **Reading Skill: Main Idea and Details** Describe three events that could lead to secondary succession.

_____

_____

_____

11. **Critical Thinking: Synthesize** How do pioneer species prepare an area for other living things?

_____

_____

12. **Inquiry Skill: Infer** An eruption doubled the size of a volcanic island. What would you expect to observe on the new land within a few months of the eruption?

_____

_____

_____

13. **Test Prep** What is the correct order in which primary succession might occur?

   A mosses   lichens   grasses   shrubs   forest

   B lichens   mosses   grasses   shrubs   forest

   C lichens   grasses   mosses   shrubs   forest

   D mosses   lichens   grasses   forest   shrubs

How Do Animals Interact in Groups?

Types of Behavior

A behavior is a response to a stimulus, such as a dog barking at a loud noise or a bird singing at a certain time of day. There are two types of behavior: innate behavior, or instinct, and learned behavior.

Innate behaviors are inherited through genes, and they don't depend on learning or experience. Seasonal behaviors such as migration and hibernation are examples of innate behaviors. Animals that inherit these traits do not have to be taught these behaviors. Some innate traits are essential to an animal's survival. Such characteristic behaviors include finding food, marking territory, courtship, and parenting. Defensive action is also an innate behavior. Defensive behavior allows animals to protect resources, including territories, from other animals. Animals defend food, mates, and offspring. Defensive behavior also helps animals protect themselves from predators. Bees, ants, and wasps inject a powerful acid into their attackers. Other animals avoid predators by making themselves hard to see. For example, a rabbit often "freezes" in the presence of a predator so that its color blends into a background of shrubs or grass. One of the most common innate defensive actions is for the prey to try to outrun its predators.

Learned behavior has been learned from experience or from observing other animals. For example, even though finding food is an innate characteristic, some animals learn more effective ways to hunt for food. Monkeys learn to use sticks to scoop ants or other insects from the ground or trees. African elephant herds are led by the oldest female elephants. Scientists suggest that the older female family members carry important knowledge, such as where to find water in a drought. These females teach younger elephants where to find the water. The younger animals learn the behavior for finding water.

Animals Form Groups

Many animals form social groups, which are collections of individuals. Groups can be composed of related individuals, such as a polar bear and her cubs. Or the group may simply be composed of individuals of a species that are in the same area at the same time, such as a flock of birds.

Sometimes animals are born into a group, such as cubs being born into a lion pride. Female lions will likely remain with their maternal pride through adulthood. Male lions will leave the maternal pride when they reach adolescence and will rejoin a pride only if they are able to displace a dominant male or coalition of males. Male lions that are related or are of similar age may form a loose group, or coalition. The group dynamics in prides and coalitions may change as dominant members, both male and female, are displaced or killed.

Other examples of animals that form social groups include animals that form herds, such as horses and elephants, animals that form flocks, such as birds, and animals that form colonies, such as bees.

17

Social Behavior

Social behavior occurs when two or more individuals interact. Social behavior usually occurs between individuals of the same species, but interspecies interactions do occur. Social behaviors have evolved to help animals deal with the complexities of living in a social group.

Individuals within a group compete with one another for limited resources. These limited resources include food, shelter, or mating privileges. This has led to the development of behaviors to express dominance and to seek reconciliation. For example, an alpha wolf may vocalize its dominance if a subordinate wolf attempts to feed on a kill first. The subordinate wolf may later seek reconciliation for the transgression by displaying meek behavior, such as turning on its back and displaying its belly. Other social groups also show a hierarchy. Groups of chickens develop a pecking order that ranks the chickens from the most dominant to the most subordinate.

Individuals within a group also show cooperative group behaviors. Wolves and lions hunt in packs to increase the chance of making a kill. Many animal groups, such as some bird or meerkat groups, use a lookout when foraging. The lookout is an individual that refrains from foraging and instead scans the area for predators. The lookout will give an alarm call if a predator is spotted. This allows most of the group to forage more efficiently. The individual acting as the lookout rotates, so all in the group are able to forage.

Other social behaviors include marking territories, courtship behaviors, parenting, and playing, which helps adolescents develop hunting and social skills.

Advantages and Disadvantages of Forming Groups

There are clear advantages to forming groups, such as decreasing predation risk and increasing hunting or foraging success. Predation risk can be decreased in groups that utilize lookouts and alarm calls. Predation risk is also decreased in groups through safety in numbers. For example, a group of meerkats will mob a snake until it is dead. The snake may be a threat to an individual meerkat, but the group is able to mount a successful defense. Animals that form large groups, such as large flocks of birds or herds of hoofed mammals, are able to dilute their predation risk. In a flock of thousands of birds, birds become prey every day. However, the odds that one particular individual will die through predation is minimal.

There are also clear disadvantages to forming groups, such as increased spread of disease or the lack of reproductive opportunities. Often, only dominant individuals in a group are allowed to reproduce successfully. When subordinate individuals break these rules, the offspring are sometimes killed or driven from the group.

How Do Animals Interact in Groups?

Write answers to the questions on the lines below.

1. What are the two types of behavior?

_____

2. What is an example of an innate defensive behavior in rabbits?

_____

3. What is an example of a learned behavior in monkeys?

_____

4. List two disadvantages to living in groups.

_____

_____

5. List two advantages to living in groups.

_____

_____

6. How do groups of chickens determine a hierarchy?

_____

7. What is a social group?

_____

8. **Main Idea** How do animals interact in groups?

_____

_____

_____

Life Science
Core Skills Science, Grade 8

9. **Vocabulary** Write a sentence using the terms *instinct* and *learned behavior*.

_____

_____

_____

10. **Reading Skill: Main Idea and Details** What is an example of cooperative behavior in animals?

_____

_____

_____

11. **Critical Thinking: Synthesis** Many humans live in groups, which are usually based on genetic relatedness. Give an example of a human group based on genetic relatedness and of a human group based on proximity, not genetic relatedness.

_____

_____

_____

12. **Inquiry Skill: Analyze** If there are disadvantages to forming groups, then why do animals still live in social groups?

_____

_____

_____

13. **Test Prep** Some lizards change color to match the plant leaf or branch on which they are sitting. This defensive behavior is called camouflage. How does this behavior help lizards survive?

   A It sharpens their hearing so they can better protect themselves.

   B It gives them a clearer view of their surroundings.

   C It provides lizards with better balance.

   D It makes the lizards hard to see by predators.

How Are Traits Inherited?

DNA and Heredity

The cells of all living things contain the molecule deoxyribonucleic acid, or DNA. DNA is the genetic material of living things and carries instructions for the organism's traits. When organisms reproduce, they pass copies of their DNA to their offspring. Passing DNA ensures that the traits of parents are passed to the offspring. This passing of traits is called heredity.

DNA is a nucleic acid composed of long chains of smaller molecules called nucleotides. A nucleotide has three parts: a sugar, a base, and a phosphate group, which contains phosphorus and oxygen atoms. DNA is a double helix molecule, which means it consists of two strands of nucleotides that spiral around each other. The structure of DNA is shown to the right.

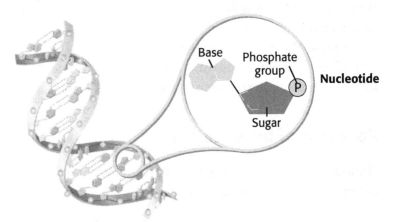

Genes and Chromosomes

Traits are passed from parents to offspring via hereditary units called genes. Genes are sections of DNA that provide instructions for the manufacture of specific proteins. A gene's instructions for making a protein are coded in the sequence of nucleotides in the gene. Therefore, the sequence of nucleotides in DNA is very important. Overall, the traits of an organism are determined by the proteins that an organism produces. All of an organism's genetic material makes up its genome.

Genes are found at particular locations on chromosomes, which are structures located in the nucleus of cells. Chromosomes are made of protein and DNA. Chromosomes contain long strands of DNA, which stores the genetic information of an organism. All members of a species have the same characteristic number of chromosomes in their body cells, much like all atoms of an element have the same characteristic number of protons in their nucleus. For example, all human body cells have 46 chromosomes. All dog body cells have 78 chromosomes.

Chromosomes within an organism can be divided into pairs, called homologous chromosomes. Homologous chromosomes carry alternate versions of a gene at the same location on each chromosome. These alternate versions are called alleles. The different alleles on homologous chromosomes contain genetic information that controls the same trait. However, the genetic information may be different. For example, the gene that controls the color of a flower is located at the same spot on both homologous chromosomes. However, one allele may provide information that results in a red flower, and one allele may provide information that results in a white flower. In organisms that reproduce through sexual reproduction, one set of chromosomes, and therefore one set of alleles, come from one parent. The other set comes from the second parent. The offspring's genome is a combination of the genome of both parents.

Mendelian Genetics

Modern genetics is based on Gregor Johann Mendel's explanations for the patterns of heredity that he studied in garden pea plants. Mendel's experiments indicated that offspring do not show a trait for every allele they receive. Instead, combinations of alleles determine traits. In a simple pattern of inheritance, a dominant allele is expressed over a recessive allele. If an organism has two recessive alleles, then the recessive trait will be expressed.

The set of alleles that an individual has for a characteristic is called the genotype. The trait that results from a set of alleles is the phenotype. In other words, genotype determines phenotype. Phenotype can also be affected by conditions in the environment, such as nutrients and temperature. If an individual has two of the same alleles of a certain gene, the individual is homozygous for the related character. On the other hand, if an individual has two different alleles of a certain gene, the individual is heterozygous for the related character. In the heterozygous case, the dominant allele is expressed.

Patterns of Inheritance

Although Mendel was correct about the inheritance of the traits he studied, most patterns of inheritance are more complex than those that Mendel identified.

An autosome is a chromosome other than an X or Y sex chromosome. If a trait is sex-linked, its effects are usually seen only in males. A sex-linked gene's allele is located only on the X or Y chromosome. Because males have only one X chromosome, a male who carries a recessive allele on the X chromosome will exhibit the sex-linked condition.

When several genes influence a character, the character exhibits polygenic inheritance. The genes for a polygenic character may be scattered along the same chromosome or located on different chromosomes. Determining the effect of any one of these genes is difficult. Familiar examples of polygenic characters in humans include eye color, height, weight, and hair and skin color.

In some organisms, an individual displays a phenotype that is intermediate between the two parents, a condition known as incomplete dominance. For example, when a snapdragon with red flowers is crossed with a snapdragon with white flowers, a snapdragon with pink flowers is produced. Neither the red nor the white allele is completely dominant over the other allele. The flowers appear pink.

Genes with three or more alleles are said to have multiple alleles. For example, in the human population, the ABO blood groups (blood types) are determined by three alleles and are therefore an example of a multiple allele pattern of inheritance.

How Are Traits Inherited?

Match each term to its correct definition.

Definitions

_____ 1. structures located in a cell nucleus that contain DNA

_____ 2. all of an organism's genes

_____ 3. characterized by phenotype that is intermediate between two parents

_____ 4. nucleic acid composed of long chains of smaller molecules called nucleotides

_____ 5. provides information for producing proteins

_____ 6. characterized by several genes influencing a character

_____ 7. alternate version of gene

Terms

a. genome

b. allele

c. gene

d. polygenic inheritance

e. DNA

f. incomplete dominance

g. chromosome

8. **Main Idea** What is heredity?

_____

_____

_____

9. **Vocabulary** Describe the difference between the *genotype* and *phenotype* of an organism.

_____

_____

_____

10. **Reading Skill: Compare and Contrast** What is the difference between a dominant allele and a recessive allele?

_____

_____

_____

11. **Critical Thinking: Synthesize** How do genes result in the expressed traits of an organism?

_____

_____

_____

12. **Inquiry Skill: Predict** What would happen if the nucleotide sequence of a gene got mixed up?

_____

13. **Test Prep** A gardener crossed a plant with red flowers with a plant that had white flowers. The offspring plants had pink flowers. What is the MOST LIKELY genetic reason for these differences in color?

   A codominance

   B recessive pink genes

   C polygenic inheritance

   D incomplete dominance

What Are Genetic Mutations?

Genetic Mutation

Although changes in an organism's hereditary information are relatively rare, they can occur. A change in the DNA of a gene is called a mutation. Mutations in gametes can be passed on to offspring of the affected individual, but mutations in body cells affect only the individual in which they occur.

Genes provide an organism's cells with the information needed to produce specific proteins. The expression of these proteins results in an individual's traits. Genetic mutations can result in a change to the structure or function of proteins. Mutations can have a beneficial, harmful, or neutral effect on an organism.

Types of Mutations

In a point mutation, a single nucleotide changes. Point mutations include insertions, deletions, and substitutions. In an insertion mutation, a nucleotide is inserted into a gene. In a deletion mutation, a nucleotide is removed from a gene, often during meiosis. In a substitution mutation, a nucleotide on a gene is replaced by a different, incorrect nucleotide. Deletions, insertions, and substitutions are not always point mutations. They can also apply to mutations that involve longer sequences of DNA.

A duplication mutation occurs when a chromosome fragment attaches to its homologous chromosome, which will then carry two copies of a certain set of genes. Another type of mutation is an inversion mutation, in which the chromosome piece reattaches to the original chromosome but in a reverse orientation. If the piece reattaches to a nonhomologous chromosome, a translocation mutation results.

Mutations that move an entire gene to a new location are called gene rearrangements. Changes in a gene's position often disrupt the gene's function because the gene is exposed to new regulatory controls in its new location.

Mutations that change a gene are called gene alterations. Gene alterations usually result in the placement of the wrong amino acid during protein assembly. This error will usually disrupt a protein's function.

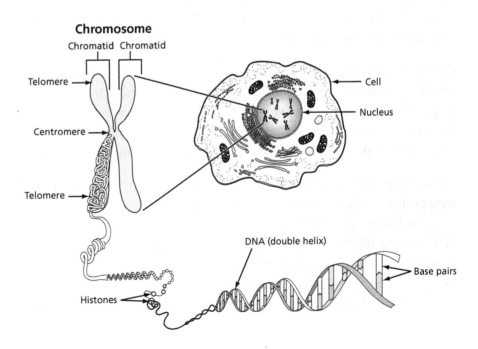

25

Effect of Mutations

Some mutations cause no change in an individual's traits. This can happen for many reasons. One reason may be that the mutation occurred in a segment of DNA that does not code for a protein. Another reason may be that the organism has the mutation only in one allele. The non-mutated allele may be able to provide the needed information to produce the correct protein.

Some mutations produce changes in traits that are beneficial to the organism, while other mutations are harmful or even lethal to the organism. For example, think about a change in the DNA that determines the color of a moth. A mutation that produces a change that helps the moth blend better with its surroundings and avoid predators would be beneficial to the moth. A mutation that makes the moth more noticeable to predators would be a harmful, or maybe lethal, mutation.

Diseases can be caused by mutations. Some are caused when a person's genetic material is damaged or copied incorrectly, resulting in genes that produce faulty proteins. Mutations can occur randomly, or they can be caused by exposure to environmental factors, such as radiation or chemicals. When a mutation occurs in the genetic material of an egg or sperm, it can be passed from parent to offspring. Harmful effects produced by inherited mutations are called genetic disorders. Examples of genetic disorders include cystic fibrosis, hemophilia, and Huntington's disease.

Importance of Mutations

Mutations are changes in DNA or chromosomes. Recall that DNA is the substance that transmits genetic information from one generation to the next. Therefore, mutations can increase genetic diversity.

In a stable environment, the amount of genetic variation in a population is not critical to the survival of the population. Individuals survive and reproduce in the same conditions generation after generation. However, when an environment changes, the amount of genetic variation among the individuals in the population can play a critical role in the survival of the population.

For example, consider a population of frogs in a pond. If the average annual temperature of the pond increases, it can affect the survival of individual frogs. If there is very little genetic diversity, and every frog in the population can live only in the same temperature range, the population of frogs might die out in response to the increased temperature of the pond water. However, suppose the frog population has a great amount of genetic diversity. Some of the frogs might be able to survive in warmer water.

Those frogs will probably survive and reproduce individuals that can also survive in the warmer temperatures. Although mutations from one allele (form of a gene) to another can eventually change allele frequencies in a population, mutation rates in nature are very slow. Most genes mutate only about 1 to 10 times per 100,0000 cell divisions, so mutation does not significantly change allele frequencies except over very long periods. Furthermore, not all mutations result in phenotypic (what the organism looks like) changes. Also, in order for a mutation to be passed along in a population, it must occur in the sex cells. Remember that mutations in body cells are not passed to the next generation.

What Are Genetic Mutations?

Write answers to the questions on the lines below.

1. What is a source of new alleles in natural populations?

   _____

2. What is an inversion mutation?

   _____

   _____

3. What information do genes provide?

   _____

4. What is a point mutation?

   _____

5. Are mutations common or rare?

   _____

6. What are two environmental factors that can cause mutations?

   _____

7. Where does a mutation have to occur for it to be passed to the next generation?

   _____

   _____

8. **Main Idea** What are genetic mutations?

   _____

   _____

   _____

9. **Vocabulary** Describe gene alterations using the terms *beneficial*, *harmful*, and *neutral*.

_____

_____

_____

10. **Reading Skill: Main Idea and Details** Why are genetic mutations important for organisms living in changing environments?

_____

_____

_____

11. **Critical Thinking: Analyze** Explain how a mutation could have no effect on the organism that inherits the mutation.

_____

_____

_____

12. **Inquiry Skill: Infer** The sequences below show two different sequences of the same gene.

Wild Type: TTGACTCGGTATAC; Mutant: TTGACTCGTATAC.

The Wild Type sequence is the original version of the gene and the Mutant sequence is the gene after a mutation. What type of mutation has occurred? Explain your answer.

_____

_____

13. **Test Prep** Which of the following mutations most likely would improve the chances that an organism would survive and reproduce?

A   a stronger scent that makes an animal easier to find

B   a weaker scent that makes a flower less attractive to bees

C   weaker eyesight that makes an animal less likely to find prey

D   stronger leg muscles that allow an animal to jump away from danger

What Is the Fossil Record?

Fossil Record

All of the fossils on Earth are part of the fossil record. The fossil record is a historical sequence of life indicated by fossils found in layers of Earth's crust. Scientists examine the fossil record to gather information about organisms that lived in Earth's past and to figure out how they relate to the organisms living on Earth today. Scientists can learn a great deal about organisms by examining the fossil record. They can determine the order in which species appeared and the period during which a species became extinct. All of this information can be used by scientists to help them determine relationships among living things.

The fossil record does not provide a complete picture of all forms of life that have lived on Earth. Many species have lived in environments where fossils do not form. Most fossils form when organisms or traces of organisms are buried very quickly in fine sediments. These sediments can be deposited by wind, water, or volcanic eruptions. Wet lowlands, slow-moving streams, lakes, shallow streams, and areas near volcanoes are the environments where fossils are most likely to form. However, even if an organism lived in these kinds of environments, the chances of its dead body forming a fossil are slim. It is more likely that the body would be eaten and scattered by scavengers than it would be covered by sediments. Another reason that the fossil record is incomplete is that the bodies of some organisms decay faster than the bodies of others. An animal with a hard skeleton, such as a crab, would have a better chance of forming a fossil than would an organism with a soft body, such as a jellyfish.

Even though the fossil record is incomplete, it provides strong evidence for the change in Earth's populations during its long history. When a fossil is discovered, scientists date it using various dating techniques. There are two types of dating techniques used for rock layers and fossils: relative dating and absolute dating.

Relative Dating

One of the most important pieces of information about a fossil is its age. How do scientists know when the organisms that formed different fossils lived? Scientists combine data from all the known undisturbed rock sequences around the world to create a geologic column. The geologic column is an ideal sequence of rock layers that contains all known fossils and rock formations on Earth, arranged from oldest to youngest. Geologists rely on the geologic column to interpret rock sequences.

What can scientists learn by examining undisturbed rock sequences, such as the one shown in the illustration? Knowing that rock layers are arranged from oldest at the bottom to newest at the top, scientists can infer that the species that appear in lower layers, such as layer A, are older than those that appear in higher layers, such as B and C. They can also determine what types of organisms lived at the same time.

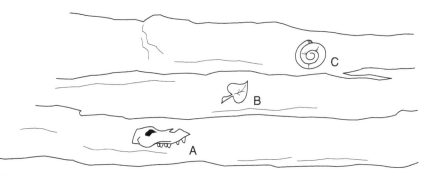

Absolute Dating

Scientists also use absolute dating to determine the age of fossils. In this process, scientists establish the age of an object by determining the number of years it has existed. Radiometric dating is the most common method of absolute dating. In the process of radioactive decay, an unstable radioactive isotope (the parent isotope) of one element breaks down into a stable isotope (the daughter isotope). The radioactive decay of a parent isotope into a stable daughter isotope can occur in a single step or series of steps. In either case, the rate of decay is constant. Therefore, to date rock, scientists compare the amount of parent material to daughter material. The more daughter material there is, the older the rock.

Once scientists know the age of a fossil, they can then place the fossil in its correct sequence among other fossils. When this is done, an orderly pattern of evolution can be seen. Then scientists can use this evidence to draw conclusions about how the organisms and populations have changed over time. By combining this information with other scientific evidence, they can infer evolutionary evidence among different kinds of organisms.

Interpreting the Fossil Record

What could you conclude if you found marine fossils on top of a mountain? The presence of marine fossils means that the rocks of the mountain formed in a totally different environment—at the bottom of an ocean. The fossil record reveals a history of environmental change. For example, marine fossils help scientists reconstruct ancient coastlines and the deepening and shallowing of ancient seas.

Using the fossils of plants and land animals, scientists can reconstruct past climates. They can tell whether the climate in an area was cooler or wetter than it is at present. At certain times during Earth's history, the number of species has increased or decreased dramatically. An increase in the number of species often comes as a result of either a relatively sudden increase or decrease in competition among species. On the other hand, the number of species decreases dramatically over a relatively short period of time during a mass extinction event. Extinction is the death of every member of a species. Gradual events, such as global climate change and changes in ocean currents, can cause mass extinctions. A combination of these events can also cause mass extinctions.

What Is the Fossil Record?

Fill in the blank.

1. During _____, the parent isotope decays into the daughter isotope.

2. The _____ is an ideal sequence of rock layers that contains fossils in order from youngest to oldest.

3. _____ is the death of every member of a species.

4. The fossil record is _____ because not every living organism has left a fossil behind.

5. Most fossils form when organisms are quickly buried in fine _____.

6. Radiometric dating is a form of _____ dating.

7. _____ dating dates a fossil based on its position with the geologic column.

8. **Main Idea** What is the fossil record?

_____

_____

Life Science
Core Skills Science, Grade 8

9. Vocabulary Write a sentence using the terms *absolute dating* and *relative dating*.

_____

_____

10. Reading Skill: Cause and Effect What conditions could cause a fossil to form?

_____

_____

_____

11. Critical Thinking: Predict Describe a situation in which a scientist could not use radiometric dating to correctly date a fossil.

_____

_____

_____

12. Inquiry Skill: Use Models Draw a diagram that models an undisturbed geologic column with five distinct layers. Provide each layer with a characteristic fossil. Label the layers from one to five, with one being the oldest layer and five being the youngest layer.

13. Test Prep Scientists have found fossils of marine animals on tops of mountains in Canada. What does this tell us about the history of that environment?

A The area was once covered by ocean sediment.

B The ancient environment did not favor fossilization.

C The ancient environment was much drier than today's environment.

D The mountains formed before the animals died.

What Is Natural Selection?

Natural Selection?

In 1859, the English naturalist Charles Darwin published convincing evidence that species evolve, and he proposed a reasonable mechanism explaining how evolution occurs. Darwin proposed that individuals that have physical or behavioral traits that better suit their environment are more likely to survive and will reproduce more successfully than those that do not have such traits. Darwin called this differential rate of reproduction natural selection. In time, the number of individuals that carry favorable characteristics that are also inherited will increase in a population. Thus, the nature of the population will change—a process called evolution.

Darwin further suggested that organisms differ from place to place because their habitats present different challenges to, and opportunities for, survival and reproduction. Each species has evolved and has accumulated adaptations in response to its particular environment. An adaptation is an inherited trait that has become common in a population because the trait provides a selective advantage. Adaptations can be anatomical, physiological, or behavioral changes. Natural selection usually leads to the increase of favorable traits in a population and the suppression of unfavorable traits.

Four Parts of Natural Selection

❶ **Overproduction** A tarantula's egg sac may hold 500–1,000 eggs. Some of the eggs will survive and develop into adult spiders. Some will not.

❷ **Genetic Variation** Every individual has its own combination of traits. Each tarantula is similar to, but not identical to, its parents.

❸ **Competition** Some tarantulas may be caught by predators, such as this wasp. Other tarantulas may starve or get a disease. Only some of the tarantulas will survive to adulthood.

❹ **Successful Reproduction** The tarantulas that are best adapted to their environment are likely to have many offspring that survive.

There are four parts to natural selection: overproduction, genetic variation, competition, and reproductive success.

Components of Natural Selection

Individuals tend to produce more offspring than the environment can support, which is overproduction. Thus, individuals of a population often compete with one another to survive and reproduce.

For natural selection to occur, a population must have genetic variation. The genetic variation of a population is a measure of how much individuals in a population differ genetically. Variation is obvious in humans in so many ways—differences in hair color or texture, eye color, height, mouth shape, or skin color—to name just a few. But variation also applies to species whose members may appear identical, such as a species of bacteria. Genetic variation is important for the survival of a species. Populations with a low genetic variation are less likely than populations with a high genetic variation to adapt to changes in their environment. Environmental factors determine which traits in a population are favorable.

The environment presents challenges to survival and successful reproduction. Organisms within a population compete with one another for limited resources. Organisms are also subject to factors such as predation and disease. Because of variation among individuals, some individuals of a population or species are better suited to survive. Naturally, an organism that does not survive to reproduce or whose offspring die before the offspring can reproduce does not pass on its genes to future generations.

Individuals that are better able to cope with the challenges presented by their environment tend to experience greater reproductive success and leave more offspring than those individuals less suited to the environment. Over time, the traits that make these individuals of a population better able to survive and reproduce tend to spread in that population.

Natural Selection Acts on a Population

It is important to note that individuals in a population often have different traits, but the individuals themselves don't evolve. Natural selection produces changes at the population level, not at the individual level. Over time, traits that are favorable to survival in the particular environment will become more frequent in the population.

Environmental factors determine which traits in a population are favorable. Different environments have different environmental factors. For example, desert environments receive very little rainfall. Organisms like the cactuses that live in a desert need to be able to survive dry conditions. But those that live in a rain forest have a different set of environmental factors; the conditions there are very wet and humid. The cactuses would not be able to survive in the rainforest.

Evolution

Evolution is a change in the genetic characteristics of a population from one generation to the next. Evolution in nature occurs through the process of natural selection. Scientists have found many different kinds of evidence that support the theory of evolution. Fossils offer the most direct evidence that evolution takes place. Evidence of orderly change can be seen when fossils are arranged according to their age. The anatomy and development of living things also shows evidence of evolution. For example, the similarities of structures in different vertebrates provide evidence that all vertebrates share a common ancestor. Biological molecules also show evolutionary relationships. Differences in amino acid sequences and DNA sequences are greater between species that are more distantly related than between species that are more closely related.

34

Name _____   Date _____

What Is Natural Selection?

Write answers to the questions on the lines below.

1. What is overproduction?

   _____

2. Who proposed the theory of evolution through natural selection?

   _____

3. What is an adaptation?

   _____

   _____

4. Why is genetic variation necessary for natural selection to occur?

   _____

   _____

5. Which type of trait will natural selection suppress: a favorable trait or an unfavorable trait?

   _____

6. What determines which traits in a population are favorable?

   _____

   _____

7. Do individuals evolve? Explain your answer.

   _____

   _____

8. **Main Idea** What is natural selection?

   _____

   _____

9. Vocabulary Write a paragraph explaining how the terms *evolution* and *natural selection* are related.

_____

_____

_____

10. Reading Skill: Text Structure What are the four components of natural selection?

_____

_____

11. Critical Thinking: Make Connections Why do the genetically-determined behaviors of individuals best adapted to survive become more common in each new generation?

_____

_____

12. Inquiry Skill: Predict There are three species of birds on an island. Bird A has a heavy bill for eating seeds. Bird B has a pointed bill for eating insects. Bird C has a sharp bill for eating insects and seeds. If all insects suddenly disappeared, which bird or birds would be least affected? Explain your answer.

_____

_____

_____

13. Test Prep Natural selection favors behavioral traits that benefit

   A the prey.

   B the population.

   C the individual.

   D the environment.

How Do New Species Form?

Evolution by Natural Selection

Separate populations of a single species often live in several different kinds of environments. In each environment, natural selection acts on the population. Natural selection results in the evolution of offspring that are better adapted to that environment. If their environments differ enough, separate populations of the same species can become very dissimilar. Over time, populations of the same species that differ genetically because of adaptations to different living conditions become what biologists call subspecies. Eventually, the subspecies may become so different that they can no longer interbreed successfully. Biologists then consider them separate species.

Speciation

In each environment, natural selection acts on the population. For example, notice in the graph how over several years the beak size of Galápagos finches varied as rainfall varied. Beak size increased in drier years because plants produced few small, tender seeds that are plentiful in wet conditions. The larger beaks that became more common after several dry years allowed the finches to dig deeper in the soil to find insects to eat. The feeding success of the birds with larger beaks enabled them to survive and produce offspring.

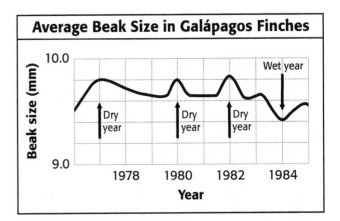

Now suppose this population of finches had been separated in 1976, and one population began living in a drier environment. Natural selection in each of the populations would result in the evolution of offspring that are better adapted to the particular environment. Over time, the population of finches that lived in the drier area would probably have more individuals with larger beaks than would the population of finches that lived in the wetter area.

If their environments differ enough and long enough, two separate populations of the same species of finches could become very dissimilar. Over time, the finches that differ genetically because of adaptations to different living conditions would become a subspecies. The members of newly formed subspecies would have taken the first step toward speciation.

Species formation takes place in stages as natural selection favors changes that increase reproductive success. Therefore, a species molded by natural selection has an improved "fit" to its environment. The accumulation of genetic differences between groups is called divergence. Divergence leads to the formation of new species. Biologists call the process by which new species form speciation.

Rate of Speciation

For decades, most biologists have understood evolution as a gradual process that occurs continuously. The model of evolution in which gradual change over a long period leads to species formation is called gradualism. But some biologists have suggested that successful species may stay unchanged for long periods. They have hypothesized that major environmental changes in the past have caused evolution to occur in spurts. This model of evolution, in which periods of rapid change in species are separated by periods of little or no change, is called punctual equilibrium.

Paleontologists, scientists who study past geologic periods, have long noticed a repeating pattern in the history of life reflected in the fossil record. Bursts of evolutionary activity are followed by long periods of stability. This pattern is described by the theory of punctuated equilibrium. Niles Eldredge and Stephen Jay Gould originally proposed this theory in 1972. It was written as a revision of Darwin's idea that new species arise through gradual transformations of ancestral species. It is important to note that the theory of punctuated equilibrium offers a revised explanation for the rate of speciation, but still involves Darwinian natural selection.

Adaptive Radiation

The diversification of one ancestral species into many descendent species is called adaptive radiation. These descendent species are usually adapted to a wide range of environments. One example of adaptive radiation is the radiation of mammals following the mass extinction at the end of the Cretaceous period 65 million years ago.

Although mammals had evolved for about 150 million years before the end of the Cretaceous period, they barely resembled the mammals we know today. The earliest mammals were tiny, usually insect eaters, and mostly nocturnal. These characteristics allowed them to coexist with the dinosaurs. The extinction of the dinosaurs left environments full of opportunities for other types of animals. In the first 10 million years following the dinosaurs' extinction, more than 4000 mammal species evolved, including whales, bats, rodents, and primates.

How Do New Species Form?

Fill in the blank.

1. _____ is the formation of a new species as a result of evolution by natural selection.

2. _____ results in the evolution of offspring that are better adapted to an environment.

3. A(n) _____ is a population of species that differs genetically due to adaptions to different living conditions.

4. Gradual change over a long period of time leading to speciation is called

   _____.

5. The accumulation of genetic differences between two groups is known as

   _____.

6. Niles Eldredge and Stephen Jay Gould originally proposed the theory of

   _____ in 1972.

7. **Main Idea** How do new species form?

   _____

   _____

   _____

   _____

   _____

8. **Vocabulary** Describe *punctuated equilibrium* and the major cause of this type of evolution.

_____

_____

_____

9. **Reading Skill: Main Idea and Details** What is one source of evidence for the theory of punctuated equilibrium?

_____

_____

10. **Critical Thinking: Synthesize** What is another example of adaptive radiation in the animal kingdom? Explain your answer.

_____

_____

11. **Inquiry Skill: Infer** How are divergence and speciation related?

_____

_____

_____

12. **Test Prep** Speciation is the formation of new species as a result of evolution by natural selection. What effect could separation of populations have on speciation?

   A One half of the species will go extinct if the population is separated.

   B The separated populations will always evolve into at least two different species.

   C If the environments differ enough, the separated populations may evolve differently.

   D By separating, the populations will no longer be able to interbreed and will die off.

How Are Stars Classified?

Hertzsprung-Russell Diagram

Almost 100 years ago, the astronomers Hertzsprung and Russell began making scatter-plot graphs that compared the luminosity of a star with its surface temperature. These efforts resulted in the Hertzsprung-Russell diagram. On this diagram, stars are not evenly distributed. Instead, many follow a waved line called the main sequence. The separate cluster of stars found above and to the right of the main sequence is labeled giants.

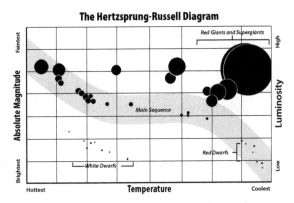

The Hertzsprung-Russell Diagram

Scientists have concluded that stars in the main sequence of a Hertzsprung-Russell diagram create heat and light by fusing hydrogen into helium. They predict that stars close to the mass of our sun can continue in their hydrogen-fusion stage for 10 billion years. More massive stars have shorter lives, and stars that are less massive than the sun have longer lives and tend to be found at the lower right of the main sequence on a Hertzsprung-Russell diagram. The upper-right section of the Hertzsprung-Russell diagram is for stars with cooler temperatures and higher luminosity.

When almost all the hydrogen is used up in a star about the size of the sun, its core contracts. Hydrogen fusion continues in the outer shell as it expands and cools. These stars begin to glow with a reddish color and are known as giants. Stars that are more massive than the sun grow even larger than giants. These stars are known as supergiants. They often become 100 or more times larger than the sun. Some stars, like Betelgeuse, grow to 1,000 times greater than the size of the sun. However, because their surface areas have expanded, their surface temperatures are relatively cool.

When a star cannot create any more energy by fusion, it will eventually shrink. Scientists predict that stars that have a mass close to the sun's will shrink until they are about the size of Earth. These stars, now called white dwarfs, will cool down over billions of years and gradually fade. However, stars more than 8 times the mass of the sun will contract into very dense neutron stars or into black holes, whose gravity is so great that not even light can escape from the star.

Stellar Composition

Astronomers use an instrument called a spectrograph to break a star's light into a spectrum. The spectrum gives astronomers information about the composition and temperature of a star. Emission lines are made when certain wavelengths of light, or colors, are given off by hot gases. When an element emits light, only some colors in the spectrum show up, while all the other colors are missing. Each element has a unique set of bright emission lines. Emission lines are like fingerprints for the elements.

Because a star's atmosphere absorbs colors of light instead of emitting them, the spectrum of a star is called an absorption spectrum. An absorption spectrum is produced when light from a hot solid or dense gas passes through a less dense, cooler gas. The cooler gas absorbs portions of the spectrum. The black lines of a star's spectrum represent portions of the spectrum that are absorbed by the atmosphere. The pattern of lines in a star's absorption spectrum shows some of the elements in the star's atmosphere. They can also help scientists deduce the temperature, density, and pressure of the gas. The sun's spectrum reveals that about 75% of the sun's mass is hydrogen, and hydrogen and helium together make up about 99% of the sun's mass. The sun's spectrum also shows that it contains traces of almost all other chemical elements.

Light Year

The stars are much farther away than the planets are. In fact, stars are so distant that a new unit of length—the light year—was created to measure their distance. A light year is a unit of length equal to the distance that light travels in 1 year. Light travels at a velocity of about 3×10^8 m/s. One light year is equal to about 9.46 trillion kilometers!

After the sun, the star closest to Earth is Proxima Centauri, located more than 4 light years away. To walk an equivalent distance, a person would have to walk around Earth more than 944 million times! Four space probes are en route to interstellar space. They are traveling at a rate of approximately 40,000 km/h. Even at this speed, it would take 150,000 years for the probes to reach Proxima Centauri.

The light year is also used to describe the size of a galaxy. For example, the Milky Way galaxy is a disc-shaped spiral galaxy about 100,000 light years across and 1,000 light years thick. The farthest objects we can observe are more than 10 billion light years away. Although the stars may appear to be at similar distances from Earth, their distances vary greatly.

Constellations

Constellations are patterns of stars visible in the night sky from Earth. Most of the official constellations recognized today date back to ancient times. If you have ever observed the sky, you have probably noticed that stars and the constellations appear to move. This is due to the rotation and revolution of Earth.

Earth experiences two types of motion. You have probably noticed at night that stars will rise in the eastern horizon and later in the evening move across the sky and are nearer the western horizon. This daily motion is due to the rotation of Earth on its axis, much like a spinning toy top. Earth rotates from west to east, making one rotation in 24 hours. This rotation makes stars, the moon, other planets, and the sun appear to us to rise in the east and set in the west. At any given moment, it is daytime on half of Earth due to the sun's illumination, and nighttime on the half of Earth that faces away from the sun.

Earth also revolves around the sun, and completes one trip in a year. The yearly orbit around the sun and Earth's 23.5° axis tilt are responsible for the yearly seasons that we experience. The revolution of Earth is also responsible for larger changes seen in the position of constellations in the night sky. For example, if a constellation is viewed in July and then again in December, it may appear as though the stars have changed position. However, we, the observers, have changed position. During the six months between July and December, Earth has moved to the opposite side of its orbit. This change of observation point makes constellations appear to have moved in the night sky.

How Are Stars Classified?

Write answers to the questions on the lines below.

1. If a star has a spectrum similar to the sun's, what is likely true of the star?

   _____

2. What is a light year?

   _____

3. What instrument breaks a star's light into a spectrum?

   _____

4. What two properties of stars does a Hertzprung-Russell diagram compare?

   _____

   _____

5. What is a constellation?

   _____

6. A star is hot and has a low luminosity. How would you classify the star using the Hertzsprung-Russell diagram?

   _____

7. What are emission lines?

   _____

   _____

8. **Main Idea** Why do stars appear to move in the night sky?

   _____

   _____

   _____

   _____

   _____

Star like the sun   Red giant   White dwarf

Earth Science
Core Skills Science, Grade 8

9. **Vocabulary** Write a paragraph describing three characteristics that scientists can use to classify stars using the terms *main sequence*, *spectrum*, and *light year*.

_____

_____

_____

_____

10. **Reading Skill: Cause and Effect** What will happen to the sun when almost all of its hydrogen is used up?

_____

_____

_____

11. **Critical Thinking: Synthesis** The sun has two major spectral lines as well as additional lines. Describe the major spectral lines and tell why the sun has the extra lines.

_____

_____

_____

12. **Inquiry Skill: Predict** What process might move a star toward the upper right section of a Hertzsprung-Russell diagram?

_____

_____

_____

13. **Test Prep** The star Aldebaran is an orange giant star. It is about 65 light years away. If Aldebaran were to explode tonight,

    A it would appear brighter than the full moon.

    B we would see the explosion right away.

    C we would not see it explode until 65 years from now.

    D it would change from orange to blue.

What Is the Earth-Moon System?

Characteristics of the Moon

The moon is a natural satellite orbiting Earth, which in turn orbits the sun. The moon is held in place around Earth due to the gravitational attraction between the two bodies. The moon has a diameter of almost 3500 kilometers (km). The moon has no atmosphere, so there is nothing to protect the moon from impacts with smaller bodies. Therefore, the surface of the moon has been shaped by continuous bombardment from smaller bodies, such as asteroids and meteoroids. These impacts are the cause of the many and massive craters on the moon. The moon's surface is covered in regolith, a combination of rock particles and dust that formed during impacts on the moon.

The dominant theory that explains the formation of the moon is the giant impact hypothesis. Scientists theorize that a large body, possible the size of a small planet, hit Earth during the final stages of its formation. The impact launched debris into orbit around Earth. The debris eventually condensed due to gravitational attraction, and the moon was formed.

Just like Earth, the moon rotates once around its internal axis each day. This is an example of synchronous rotation, which occurs when an orbiting body has a similar period of rotation as the body being orbited. Synchronous rotation is the reason that only one side of the moon is ever visible from Earth.

Phases of the Moon

From Earth, one of the most noticeable aspects of the moon is its continually changing appearance. In 28 days, the moon's earthward face changes from a fully lit circle to a thin crescent and then back to a circle. These different appearances of the moon result from its changing position relative to Earth and the sun.

As the moon revolves around Earth, the amount of sunlight on the side of the moon that faces Earth changes. The different appearances of the moon due to its changing position are called phases. The phases of the moon are shown in the figure.

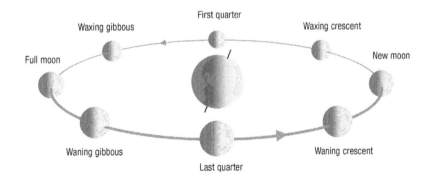

First quarter

Waxing gibbous

Waxing crescent

Full moon

New moon

Waning gibbous

Waning crescent

Last quarter

When the moon is waxing, the sunlit fraction that we can see from Earth is getting larger. When the moon is waning, the sunlit fraction is getting smaller. Notice in the figure that even as the phases of the moon change, the total amount of sunlight that the moon gets remains the same. Half the moon is always in sunlight, just as half of Earth is always in sunlight. But because the moon's period of rotation is the same as its period of revolution, on Earth you always see the same side of the moon. If you lived on the far side of the moon, you would see the sun for half of each lunar day, but you would never see Earth!

The Earth-Moon System

A system is a set of connected parts that form a more complex whole. Earth and the moon are part of the Earth-moon system. Earth and the moon orbit each other, and the reactions between the gravitational and magnetic fields of both bodies affect Earth in many ways.

First, Earth rotates around its internal axis once each day. According to the National Aeronautics and Space Administration (NASA), the presence of the moon helps to minimize the "wobble" of Earth on its axis. This leads to a more stable climate, since a shift in Earth's axis can cause warming and cooling trends.

The moon also produces tides on Earth. Tides are daily changes in the level of ocean water along a coast. Tides are influenced by the gravitational pull of the sun and the moon, though the moon's pull is the main influence on tides. During high tide, a bulge in the ocean water on the side of Earth nearest the moon appears. A bulge or high tide also occurs simultaneously on the opposite side of Earth due to the combined motions of Earth and the moon that "throw" or push water to the side opposite the moon as Earth spins. As water moves outward into the bulges, low places are also formed, resulting in low tides. Tides are very regular, and people track tides to aid recreational boaters and professional maritime vessels.

Astronomers have spent thousands of years studying the moon. In 1969, Neil Armstrong was the first person to walk on the moon. He was part of NASA's Apollo 11 mission, which successfully landed on and returned from the moon. Further exploration of the moon is part of NASA's long-term plans for exploring the solar system. The moon can be used as a staging area and laboratory to set up and test future space exploration technology, such as habitation modules, landing vehicles, and resource mining equipment.

What Is the Earth-Moon System?

Fill in the blank.

1. The moon completes a full cycle through all its phases once every _____ days.

2. The force of _____ prevents the moon from moving away from Earth.

3. _____ is a combination of rock particles and dust that covers the surface of the moon.

4. _____ rotation is the reason that only one side of the moon is ever visible from Earth.

5. The moon causes _____ on Earth, which are daily changes in the level of ocean water.

6. _____ was the first person to walk on the moon.

7. The moon has a diameter of _____ kilometers.

8. **Main Idea** What is the Earth-Moon system?

   _____

   _____

9. **Vocabulary** Write a paragraph describing the appearance of the moon from Earth. Use the terms *synchronous rotation* and *phases of the moon*.

   _____

   _____

   _____

   _____

   _____

   _____

10. Reading Skill: Compare and Contrast Compare what is happening to the sunlit part of a waxing moon and a waning moon.

_____

_____

_____

_____

11. Critical Thinking: Evaluate What are two stabilizing factors that the moon provides for Earth?

_____

_____

_____

12. Inquiry Skill: Use Models For a science fair, you want to use two different balls to make a model of the moon orbiting Earth. The diameter of the ball that will represent Earth will be about 62 cm. You want your model to be to scale. If the moon is about 4 times smaller than Earth, what should be the diameter of the ball that represents the moon, in centimeters?

_____

_____

13. Test Prep Which of the following tells phases of the moon in order, beginning with a full moon?

A full, waning gibbous, first quarter, waxing crescent, new

B full, waning gibbous, new, waxing crescent, first quarter

C full, waxing crescent, new, waning gibbous, first quarter

D full, waxing crescent, waning gibbous, new, first quarter

How Does Gravity Cause Tides?

The Earth-Moon-Sun System

Earth is located in a solar system in the spiral-shaped Milky Way galaxy. Earth orbits the sun, a medium-sized yellow star, along with seven other planets. The moon orbits Earth. All objects are attracted to each other through gravitational force. It is gravity that holds an orbiting object in orbit. Earth's gravity holds the moon in orbit, and the sun's gravity holds the Earth in orbit. The sun's gravity also holds everything else in the solar system together. The Earth, moon and sun make up the Earth-moon-sun system. The interactions of this system cause many phenomena that can be tracked and recorded, such as the day and night and seasons on Earth, the phases of the moon, and even the motion of tides.

Tides and Gravitational Attraction

The periodic rise and fall of the water level in the oceans is called the tide. High tide is when the water level is highest. Low tide is when the water level is lowest. In the late 1600s, Isaac Newton identified the force that causes the rise and fall of tides along coastlines. According to Newton's law of gravitation, the gravitational pull of the moon on Earth and Earth's waters is the major cause of tides. The sun also causes tides, but they are smaller because the sun is much farther from Earth than the moon is.

As the moon revolves around Earth, the moon exerts a gravitational pull on the entire Earth. However, because the force of the moon's gravity decreases with increased distance between the two bodies, the gravitational pull of the moon is strongest on the side of Earth that is nearest to the moon. As a result, the ocean on Earth's near side bulges slightly, which causes a high tide within the area of the bulge.

At the same time, another tidal bulge forms on the opposite side of Earth. This tidal bulge forms because the solid Earth, which acts as though all of its mass were at Earth's center, is pulled more strongly toward the moon than the ocean water on Earth's far side. The result is a smaller tidal bulge on Earth's far side. Low tides form halfway between the two high tides. Low tides form because as ocean water flows toward the areas of high tide, the water level in other areas of the oceans drops.

Because there are two tidal bulges, most locations in the ocean have two high tides and two low tides daily. The difference in levels of ocean water at high tide and low tide is called the tidal range. The tidal range can vary widely from place to place. Because the moon rises about 50 minutes later each day, the times of high and low tides are about 50 minutes later each day.

Tides and the Phases of the Moon

The sun's gravitational pull can add to or subtract from the moon's influence on the tides. During the first- and third-quarter phases of the moon, the moon and the sun are at right angles to each other in relation to Earth. The gravitational forces of the sun and moon work against each other. As a result, the daily tidal range is small. Tides that occur during this time are called neap tides.

During the new moon and the full moon, the Earth, sun, and moon are aligned. The combined gravitational pull of the sun and the moon results in higher high tides and lower low tides. So, the daily tidal range is greatest during the new moon and the full moon. During these two monthly periods, tides are called spring tides.

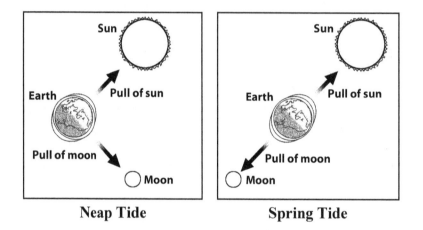

Neap Tide   **Spring Tide**

Tidal Energy

Tides can generate electricity similar to the way that hydroelectric plants on rivers generate electricity. A dam is built across an inlet. As the tide ebbs and flows, water moves in and out, turning turbines to drive electric generators. These structures are known as tidal barrages. Tidal energy can also be produced through underwater turbines that are turned by the action of waves.

Tidal energy is considered renewable energy since the oceans are vast and the ocean water is not used up, and the tides are a constant feature of the Earth-moon-sun system.

How Does Gravity Cause Tides?

Fill in the blank.

1. Earth is located in the _____ galaxy.

2. Tide are at their highest during _____ tide.

3. A(n) _____ can generate electricity from tides similar to the way hydroelectric dams on rivers generate electricity.

4. The periodic rise and fall of the water level in the oceans is called the _____.

5. Most locations in the ocean have _____ high tides and two low tides daily.

6. Low tides form halfway between the two _____ tides.

7. _____ tides form because as ocean water flows toward the areas of high tide, the water level in other areas of the ocean drops.

8. **Main Idea** What is the Earth-moon-sun system?

_____

_____

_____

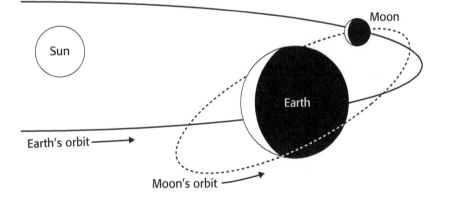

Earth Science
Core Skills Science, Grade 8

9. **Vocabulary** Write a sentence about tidal energy using the terms *tidal barrage* and *turbine*.

_____

_____

10. **Reading Skill: Main Idea and Details** What are some effects of the Earth-moon-sun system that can be studied and tracked from Earth?

_____

_____

_____

11. **Critical Thinking: Analyze** Would you classify tides as a nonrenewable or renewable energy resource? Explain.

_____

_____

_____

12. **Inquiry Skill: Synthesize** What is the angle, in degrees, between the sun, moon, and Earth during a neap tide? Explain your answer.

_____

_____

_____

13. **Test Prep** Why does the sun have a smaller gravitational effect on Earth's tides than the moon?

    A The sun is farther from Earth than the moon is.

    B The sun has less mass than the moon.

    C The sun produces less energy than the moon.

    D The sun has less volume than the moon.

How Do Seasons Affect Plants and Animals?

Seasons on Earth

In most places in the United States, the year consists of four seasons—winter, spring, summer, and fall. Seasons are periods of time characterized by a particular circumstance or feature; for instance, a particular kind of weather. Areas near the equator do not have seasonal changes. These areas have approximately the same temperatures and same amount of daylight year round.

Seasons happen because Earth is tilted on its axis at a 23.5° angle. This tilt affects how much solar energy an area receives as Earth moves around the sun. The figure below shows how latitude and the tilt of Earth affect the amount of solar energy hitting Earth's surface. The varying amounts of solar energy hitting Earth's surface cause the seasons.

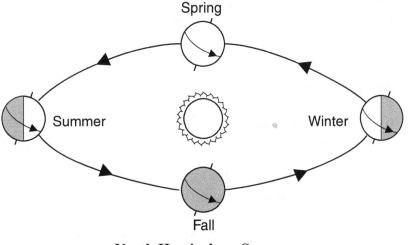

North Hemisphere Seasons

Seasons Differ by Hemisphere

The equator is an imaginary line that divides the planet into two halves. The half to the north of the equator is the Northern Hemisphere, and the half to the south of the equator is the Southern Hemisphere. During summer in the Northern Hemisphere, locations in the Northern Hemisphere experience warmer temperatures and a greater number of daylight hours because the Northern Hemisphere is tilted toward the sun and receives more-direct solar energy. At the same time, the Southern Hemisphere has colder temperatures and fewer daylight hours because it is tilted away from the sun and receives much less concentrated solar energy. It is important to note that Earth maintains the 23.5° tilt as it orbits the sun; therefore, its axis is pointing toward the North Star, also known as Polaris, at all times during its yearly revolution around the sun.

During winter in the Northern Hemisphere, the Southern Hemisphere has higher temperatures and a greater number of daylight hours because it is tilted toward the sun and receives more-direct solar energy. At that time, the Northern Hemisphere has lower temperatures and fewer daylight hours because it is tilted away from the sun and receives less-concentrated solar energy. The figure above shows the Northern Hemisphere seasons. Notice how latitude and the tilt of the Earth determine the seasons and the length of the day in a particular area.

Plant Responses to Seasons

What would happen if a plant living in an area that has very cold winters flowered in December? The plant's flowers would likely freeze and die. The flowers would never produce mature seeds. Plants living in regions with cold winters can detect the change in seasons. How do plants do this? As fall and winter approach, the days get shorter, and the nights get longer. The opposite happens when spring and summer approach. Plants respond to the change in the length of day.

The difference between day length and night length is an important environmental stimulus for many plants. This stimulus can cause plants to begin reproducing. For example, some plants flower in fall or winter. At this time, night length is long. These plants are called short-day plants. Other plants flower in spring or early summer, when night length is short. These plants are called long-day plants.

Dormancy in plants is a way for plants to avoid unsuitable conditions. When a plant is dormant, it stops growing and decreases other activities. Dormancy in plants and seeds can be triggered by decreasing temperatures, decreasing length of day, or decreasing water availability. All of these are seasonal changes that affect plants.

Seasonal Behaviors in Animals

Animals can respond to seasons just like plants. Seasonal behaviors such as migration, hibernation, and estivation are innate behaviors that some animals display in response to seasonal changes.

Migration is a yearly movement of animals over relatively long distances. Animals typically migrate in search of better conditions or more resources during difficult times in an ecosystem. This could include summer or winter seasons depending upon the area. Migration can be considered a round trip. A migration involves leaving one area due to unsuitable conditions, traveling to a second area that is more suitable, and then returning to the first area once conditions have improved. Monarch butterflies famously migrate south each year to sites in California and Mexico. The butterflies return north once winter is over.

Some animals do not leave a habitat just because conditions become unsuitable due to such factors as cold temperatures and scarce food during winter. Instead, some animals may hibernate to survive the winter. Animals that hibernate find a warm, safe den and then enter a state of torpor that is characterized by a low body temperature and heart rate. These decreased body conditions can allow an animal to survive for a longer period of time on stored energy.

Estivation is similar to hibernation, except it occurs in response to hot conditions and scarce water in the summer season. Animals also enter a state of torpor during estivation in order to conserve energy and resources. Estivation and hibernation in animals can be triggered by changes in the length of day, just as plants respond to changes in length of day.

Many animals also depend on seasonal cues for other yearly milestones, such as the beginning of mating seasons or to signal when to grow or shed a heavy winter coat.

Name _____ Date _____

How Do Seasons Affect Plants and Animals?

Match each definition to its term.

Definitions

_____ 1. period of time characterized by a certain circumstance, such as weather conditions

_____ 2. the north star

_____ 3. state of torpor entered into during the summer season

_____ 4. experiences the winter season as the Northern Hemisphere is experiencing the summer season

_____ 5. yearly movement of animals over long distances

_____ 6. state of torpor entered into during the winter season

_____ 7. half of planet to the north of the equator

Terms

a. Northern Hemisphere

b. Southern Hemisphere

c. migration

d. estivation

e. hibernation

f. season

g. Polaris

Write the answer to the question on the lines below.

8. **Main Idea** How do seasons affect plants and animals?

_____

_____

_____

_____

_____

_____

_____

9. **Vocabulary** Write a sentence using the terms *estivation* and *hibernation*.

_____

_____

10. **Reading Skill: Compare and Contrast** Explain the difference between short-day plants and long-day plants.

_____

_____

_____

11. **Critical Thinking: Analyze** Why don't locations near the equator experience all four seasons?

_____

_____

_____

12. **Inquiry Skill: Make Connections** Which seasonal response in plants is similar to a seasonal behavior displayed by animals? Explain your answer.

_____

_____

_____

13. **Test Prep** Why do we have seasons on Earth?

   A Earth is closer to the sun during summer and farther from the sun during winter.

   B The tilt of Earth's axis varies from 0° and 23.5°, which causes summer when Earth is tilted more and winter when it is straight up.

   C Seasons are caused by the moon's gravitational influence on Earth's oceans.

   D When Earth rotates around the sun, the axis remains pointed toward Polaris, giving the two hemispheres alternating periods of more and less direct solar energy.

How Are Materials Dated?

Relative Dating

Using a few basic principles, scientists can determine the order in which rock layers formed. Once they know the order, a relative age can be determined for each rock layer. Relative age indicates that one layer is older or younger than another layer but does not indicate the rock's age in years. To determine relative age, scientists usually study sedimentary rocks, using the law of superposition to determine the relative ages of the rocks. The law of superposition states that an undisturbed sedimentary rock layer is older than the layers above it and younger than the layers below it. Relative age can also be applied to fossils occurring within the rock layer.

Sedimentary rocks form when rocks break into smaller pieces, and those pieces become cemented together. Sedimentary rock, igneous rock, and metamorphic rock can all change into new sedimentary rock when sediments are weathered and eroded and then compressed and cemented together. This orderly formation of sedimentary rock makes it ideal for relative dating.

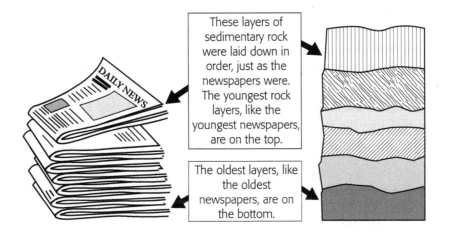

These layers of sedimentary rock were laid down in order, just as the newspapers were. The youngest rock layers, like the youngest newspapers, are on the top.

The oldest layers, like the oldest newspapers, are on the bottom.

Index Fossils

Scientists can use fossils to determine the ages of rock layers. Fossils that occur only in rock layers of a particular geologic age are called index fossils. To be an index fossil, a fossil must first be present in rocks scattered over a large region. Second, it must have features that distinguish it from other fossils. Third, the organisms from which the fossil formed must have lived during a short span of geologic time. Fourth, the fossil must occur in fairly large numbers within the rock layer.

Scientists can use index fossils to determine the ages of specific rock layers. Because organisms that formed index fossils lived during short spans of geologic time, the rock layer in which an index fossil was discovered can be dated accurately.

Radiometric Dating

Relative age indicates only that one rock layer is younger or older than another rock layer. Scientists often need to determine the numeric age, or absolute age, of rocks. Some rocks contain small amounts of radioactive material that can act as natural clocks. Atoms of the same element that have different numbers of neutrons are called isotopes. Radioactive isotopes have nuclei that emit particles and energy at a constant rate. This process is called decay. The original isotope, or parent isotope, decays into a new isotope, or daughter isotope. Different radioactive atoms have different rates at which they decompose. Scientists use this breakdown of isotopes to measure the absolute age of rocks. The method of using radioactive decay to measure absolute age is called radiometric dating.

A radioactive material's half-life is the amount of time for one-half of the parent isotope to convert to the daughter isotope. Decay rates vary in different isotopes but are always the same for the same isotope. This material decays within the rock at a constant rate. Scientists can measure the concentrations of the parent isotope and the daughter isotope and compare these concentrations to the decay rate of this radioactive material.

Radioactive Isotopes

The isotope carbon-14, 14C, is often used to date organic material, like wood, bones, and shells. It has a relatively short half-life, so it is best used for dating materials that are less than 70,000 year old. The table below shows other parent/daughter isotope combinations, the half-life, and the date range within which materials can be effectively dated. Isotopes with a longer half-life are used to date older materials. This is because the longer the half-life, the more time it takes for the concentration of the daughter isotope to build up to a level that will provide accurate results.

Radiometric Dating Methods

Radiometric dating method	Parent isotope	Daughter isotope	Half-life	Effective dating range
Radiocarbon dating	carbon-14, ^{14}C	nitrogen 14, ^{14}N	5,730 years	less than 70,000 years
Argon-argon dating, ^{39}Ar/^{40}Ar	potassium-40, ^{40}K irradiated to form argon-39, ^{39}Ar	argon-40, ^{40}Ar	1.25 billion years	10,000 to 4.6 billion years
Potassium-argon dating, ^{40}K/^{40}Ar	potassium-40, ^{40}K	argon-40, ^{40}Ar	1.25 billion years	50,000 to 4.6 billion years
Rubidium-strontium dating, ^{87}Rb/^{87}Sr	rubidium-87, ^{87}Rb	strontium-87, ^{87}Sr	48.8 billion years	10 million to 4.6 billion years
Uranium-lead dating, ^{235}U/^{207}Pb	uranium-235, ^{235}U	lead-207, ^{207}Pb	704 million years	10 million to 4.6 billion years
Uranium-lead dating, ^{238}U/^{206}Pb	uranium-238, ^{238}U	lead-206, ^{206}Pb	4.5 billion years	10 million to 4.6 billion years
Thorium-lead dating	thorium-232, ^{232}Th	lead-208, ^{208}Pb	14.0 billion years	greater than 200 million years

How Are Materials Dated?

Fill in the blank.

1. _____ rocks form when rocks break into smaller pieces and those pieces become cemented together.

2. The isotope _____ is used to date organic material.

3. Atoms of the same element that have different numbers of _____ are called isotopes.

4. Numeric age is also known as _____ age.

5. Radioactive _____ have nuclei that emit particles and energy at a constant rate.

6. A(n) _____ isotope decays into a(n) _____ isotope.

7. _____ is used to estimate numeric age.

8. **Main Idea** Explain the relationship between the law of superposition and relative dating.

_____

_____

_____

_____

Hydrogen and Two Isotopes

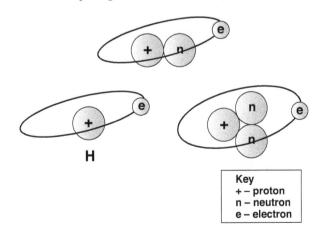

Key
+ – proton
n – neutron
e – electron

9. Vocabulary Use the terms *isotopes* and *radiometric dating* in a sentence.

_____

_____

10. Reading Skill: Main Idea and Details What four things must be true for a fossil to be considered an index fossil?

_____

_____

_____

_____

11. Critical Thinking: Evaluate How does the half-life of an isotope affect the accuracy of the radiometric dating method?

_____

_____

_____

12. Inquiry Skill: Infer Scientists have determined that Earth is over 4 billion years old. Which isotope did they most likely use to make this determination? Explain.

_____

_____

_____

_____

13. Test Prep Which is an example of absolute age?

   A A girl is younger than her brother but older than her sister.

   B A girl is 14 years old in September.

   C A boy was born before the last presidential election.

   D A boy is younger than 17, but older than 14.

What Is Evidence of Tectonic Plate Movement?

Continental Drift

Have you ever looked at a map of the world and noticed that the coastlines of continents on opposite sides of the oceans appear to fit together like the pieces of a puzzle? This observation led some scientists to reason that the continents were once joined together and had somehow drifted apart. They found evidence to support their ideas but couldn't explain how the continents had separated. German scientist Alfred Wegener first proposed the idea of continental drift in 1912. He used fossils as evidence to support his hypothesis, showing that the same species often lived on separate continents. Other evidence that helped support Wegener's hypothesis came from the alignment of mountains on different continents and fossils showing climatic changes.

The idea that the continents were once joined together was not new in Wegener's time. In 1620, Francis Bacon noted that the continents seemed to fit together, but no one could understand how they moved. In 1910, an American geologist named Frank Taylor pointed out geologic similarities between South America and Africa. Wegener's studies in 1915 were the first exhaustive research on the topic and combined evidence from many disciplines. Neither Wegener nor Taylor could explain how the continents had separated, and their observations were dismissed. It was not until the discovery of sea-floor spreading that the continental drift hypothesis was accepted.

Scientists studying the Mid-Atlantic Ridge found evidence indicating that rocks closer to the ridge are younger than rocks farther from the ridge. Scientists also learned that the ocean floor is very young. In the late 1950s, a geologist named Harry Hess suggested a new hypothesis. He suggested that magma from deep inside Earth rises to fill the crack in the center of a mid-ocean ridge. As the ocean floor moves away from the ridge, rising magma cools and solidifies to form new rock that replaces the ocean floor. This process is called sea-floor spreading. Hess suggested that if the ocean floor is moving, the continents might be moving, too.

Other Evidence Supporting the Theory of Plate Tectonics

After sea-floor spreading was discovered in the 1960s, research groups tested Wegener's hypothesis using as many methods as possible. For example, radiometric dating methods showed that rocks in corresponding parts of Africa and South America formed at the same time. This supports the idea that the coastlines were once joined.

Also, the dating of igneous rocks around mid-ocean ridges showed a symmetrical pattern, in which older rocks were located farther away from the rifts. Few rocks older than 180 million years were discovered on the ocean floor. This supports the idea that oceanic lithosphere is continuously recycled through the production of new ocean floor at mid-ocean ridges and the destruction of ocean floor at ocean trenches.

One other piece of evidence to support the theory of plate tectonics was found on the ocean floor. Scientists found that zones of magnetic reversals also followed a symmetrical pattern on either side of mid-ocean ridges. The pattern of reversals matched the pattern revealed by the ages of the rocks. This further supports the idea that older oceanic lithosphere is farther from mid-ocean ridges and younger oceanic lithosphere is closer to mid-ocean ridges.

Plate Tectonics

By the 1960s, scientists had developed the theory of plate tectonics. This theory states that Earth's crust and rigid upper mantle form the lithosphere. The lithosphere is divided into huge slabs of rocks called tectonic plates. The lithosphere lies above the asthenosphere. The solid rock of the asthenosphere flows very slowly because of density differences caused by the outward flow of heat from deep within Earth. When rock is heated, it expands, becomes less dense, and tends to rise to the surface of Earth. As the rock gets near the surface, it cools, becomes denser, and tends to sink. This process is called a convection current. Convection currents cause the slow movement of tectonic plates in the lithosphere.

Tectonic plates move around Earth's surface at rates of millimeters to centimeters per year. Plate boundaries are zones of geologic activity at the surface of Earth, where plates can separate from each other, collide with each other, and move past each other. The forces generated by these plate motions are responsible for mountain building, earthquakes, and volcanoes.

Results of Tectonic Plate Movement

Tectonic plates can also be described as objects in constant motion. The North American plate moves at a rate of about 5 cm/year. However, plate tectonics is a demolition derby of sorts, and over time plates collide, causing unbalanced forces on the moving plates. Collisions of Earth's tectonic plates are responsible for the formation of such crustal features as the Himalayan and Appalachian mountain ranges. The formation of mountain ranges is known as mountain building.

Most earthquakes take place near tectonic plate boundaries, where plates either collide, separate, or slide past one another. Tectonic plates move in different directions and at different speeds. As a result of these movements, numerous features called faults exist in Earth's crust. Earthquakes occur along faults at tectonic plate boundaries.

Volcanism is the eruption of molten rock onto the surface. About 80% of active volcanoes on land form where plates collide, and about 15% form where plates separate. The remaining few occur far from tectonic plate boundaries. Volcanoes are areas of Earth's surface through which magma and volcanic gases pass. The explosive pressure of a volcanic eruption can turn an entire mountain into a billowing cloud of ash and rock in a matter of seconds. But eruptions are also creative forces—they help form fertile farmland. They also create some of the largest mountains on Earth. During an eruption, molten rock, or magma, is forced to Earth's surface. Magma that flows onto Earth's surface is called lava.

What Is Evidence of Tectonic Plate Movement?

Fill in the blank.

1. Alfred Wegener first proposed the idea of _____ in 1912.

2. _____ currents cause the slow movement of tectonic plates in the lithosphere.

3. New ocean floor is produced at _____.

4. Ocean floor is destroyed at _____.

5. Earthquakes occur along _____ at tectonic plate boundaries.

6. The North American plate moves at a rate of about _____ centimeters per year.

7. _____ is the eruption of molten rock onto the surface.

8. **Main Idea** Correctly state the theory of plate tectonics.

_____

_____

_____

Tectonic Plates

Eurasian Plate

North American Plate

Arabian Plate

Indian Plate

Philippine Plate

Juan de Fuca Plate

Caribbean Plate

Pacific Plate

Cocos Plate

African Plate

Nazca Plate

Australian Plate

Pacific Plate

South American Plate

Scotia Plate

Antarctic Plate

9. **Vocabulary** Write a paragraph describing the results of tectonic plate movement. Use the terms *mountain building*, *volcanism*, and *earthquake*.

_____

_____

_____

_____

10. **Reading Skill: Main Idea and Details** How do convection currents cause the motion of tectonic plates?

_____

_____

_____

_____

11. **Critical Thinking: Synthesis** What are three lines of evidence that are used to support continental drift and the theory of plate tectonics?

_____

_____

_____

_____

12. **Inquiry Skill: Use Numbers** Tectonic plates move very slowly. If a tectonic plate moves 3 centimeters (cm) per year, how long in years would it take for the plate to move 3 meters (m)?

_____

_____

_____

13. **Test Prep** What can you conclude about rocks found in the center of a mid-ocean ridge?

   A They are about the same age as rocks found farther from the ridge.

   B They are older than rocks found farther from the ridge.

   C They formed more recently than rocks farther from the ridge.

   D They are more likely to have been formed by earthquakes.

What Are Ocean Currents?

Ocean Characteristics

Due to the large amount of water on Earth, it is known as an ocean planet. Over 70% of Earth's surface is covered by a connected body of water known as the global ocean. The continents on Earth are surrounded by the global ocean, which can be divided into smaller bodies of water, such as the Pacific Ocean, the Atlantic Ocean, the Indian Ocean, and the Arctic Ocean. Oceans absorb large amounts of thermal energy from the sun. This energy is distributed around Earth by ocean currents. Ocean currents also transport nutrients and debris.

Ocean water is not freshwater. It contains many dissolved substances, the most common of which is sodium chloride, or table salt. This is why ocean water is referred to as saltwater. Salinity is a measure of the concentration of dissolved salts in water. Salinity is an important characteristic of oceans that can impact the circulation of ocean water.

Ocean water contains stream-like movements of water called ocean currents. While winds are often responsible for ocean currents, the sun is the initial energy source of the winds and currents. Because the sun heats Earth more in some places than in others, convection currents are formed. These currents transfer thermal energy. With knowledge of ocean currents, people are able to predict where objects in the open ocean will be carried.

Surface Ocean Currents

Surface currents are wind-driven currents in the ocean. They moderate the climate of nearby land masses. For example, warm surface currents flow toward the poles and carry warm, equatorial waters to higher latitudes. Coastal areas near these warm surface currents tend to have warmer climates than areas farther inland at the same latitude. Cold surface currents flow from higher latitudes toward the equator and carry cold waters to tropical regions. Areas near these cold surface currents have cooler climates than areas farther inland at the same latitude. Some surface currents vary seasonally due to seasonal changes in Earth's atmosphere.

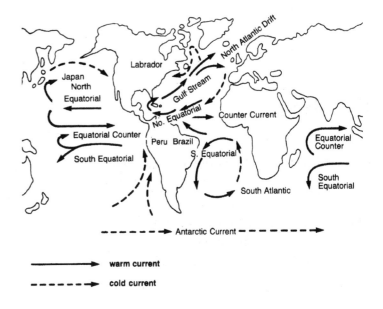

Earth Science
Core Skills Science, Grade 8

Deep Ocean Currents

Deep ocean currents are driven by differences in the temperature and salinity of ocean water. For this reason, deep ocean currents are also known as thermohaline currents (thermo: temperature, haline: salt). The temperature and salinity of ocean water ultimately affect the density of ocean water.

Density is mass per volume of a substance. Water with a higher salinity is denser than water with a lower salinity. And cold water is denser than warm water. So cold water or water with higher salinity will sink, and warm water or water with lower salinity will rise. This displacement of surface ocean water by deeper ocean water creates deep ocean currents. The illustration below shows the major deep ocean currents. These currents form a sort of "conveyor belt" that cycles deep ocean water and surface ocean water. As denser surface water sinks in the northern Atlantic Ocean, deeper water is displaced. The displaced water travels as a deep current. The temperature and salinity of the water change as it travels. Eventually, the current will rise to the surface to displace water that is colder or more saline.

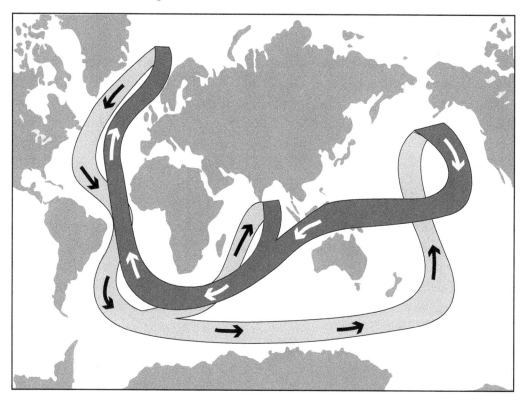

Upwelling

Another type of water movement in oceans is upwelling. Upwelling often occurs along coastlines where wind pushes surface water that is then replaced by deeper water. The deeper water that rises to the surface is usually colder with more nutrients. Successful fisheries often occur near upwellings due to this increase in nutrients.

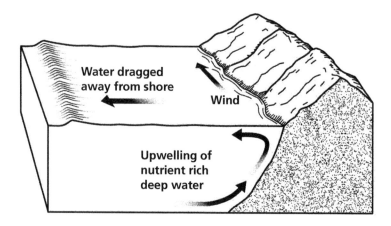

Water dragged away from shore

Wind

Upwelling of nutrient rich deep water

What Are Ocean Currents?

Write answers to the questions on the lines below.

1. What is salinity?

   _____

   _____

2. Why is Earth referred to as an ocean planet?

   _____

3. What is upwelling?

   _____

   _____

4. What are the names of four oceans on Earth?

   _____

5. What do ocean currents transport besides water?

   _____

6. Why do successful fisheries sometimes occur near upwellings?

   _____

   _____

7. Is ocean water freshwater or saltwater?

   _____

8. **Main Idea** What are ocean currents?

   _____

   _____

   _____

9. **Vocabulary** Write a sentence describing thermohaline currents using the terms *salinity* and *temperature*.

_____

_____

_____

10. **Reading Skill: Compare and Contrast** How are surface ocean currents and deep ocean currents alike and how are they different?

_____

_____

_____

11. **Critical Thinking: Analyze** In your own words, explain why water with a higher salinity is denser than water with a lower salinity.

_____

_____

_____

12. **Inquiry Skill: Predict** How might global climate change affect ocean currents?

_____

_____

_____

13. **Test Prep** The initial source of energy for ocean currents is

    A the sun

    B the rotation of Earth

    C the moon's gravity

    D continental deflections

What Affects Earth's Climate?

Climatology is the study of climates, including past, present, and future climates. Climate refers to the average weather conditions of an area over a period of time. The size of the area and the period of time change depending upon the climate being discussed. For example, if scientists wanted to study the climate of the United States from 1800 to 2000, they would study only climactic data from this time span.

Earth's climate arises from interactions between all of Earth's systems, including the atmosphere, the geosphere, the hydrosphere, the cryosphere, and the biosphere. Conditions in the atmosphere are typically used to describe weather and climate. These conditions include temperature, air pressure, wind, and precipitation.

Atmospheric Conditions

Earth's climate is primarily driven by the sun. Without sunlight, Earth would be cold and dark, and life as we know it would not exist. Energy from the sun is absorbed by the atmosphere, by landmasses, and by the oceans. A measure of this energy is temperature, and temperature is one of the most frequently reported conditions on Earth.

The sun's energy creates wind. Wind is the movement of air caused by difference in air pressure. The greater the pressure difference, the faster the wind moves. Differences in air pressure are generally caused by unequal heating of Earth. The equator receives more direct solar energy than other latitudes, so air at the equator is warmer and less dense than the surrounding air. Warm, less dense air rises and creates an area of low pressure. This warm, rising air flows toward the poles. At the poles, the air is colder and denser than the surrounding air, so it sinks. As the cold air sinks, it creates areas of high pressure around the poles. This cold polar air then flows toward the equator. This cycle of warm air rising and cool air sinking causes a circular movement of air called a convection current. These large convection currents affect climate around the planet.

Precipitation is water that falls from the atmosphere and reaches Earth's surface. Precipitation refers to liquid water (rain) or solid water (snow, hail). Gaseous water (water vapor) in the atmosphere is also reported as an atmospheric condition as humidity.

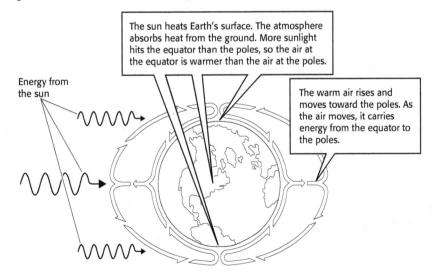

The sun heats Earth's surface. The atmosphere absorbs heat from the ground. More sunlight hits the equator than the poles, so the air at the equator is warmer than the air at the poles.

The warm air rises and moves toward the poles. As the air moves, it carries energy from the equator to the poles.

Energy from the sun

Climate Controlling Factors

Many related factors control the climate of a given area. These factors include the latitude, altitude, ocean currents, and land cover of the region.

The amount of direct solar energy a particular area receives is determined by latitude. This in turn affects the climate by controlling temperature. The figure below shows how the curve of Earth affects the amount of direct solar energy at different latitudes. Altitude also affects the temperature of a region. As altitude increases, temperature decreases. This controls climate, as well.

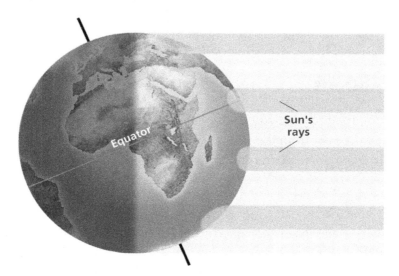

Oceans absorb and release solar energy. Ocean currents redistribute energy around Earth. Ocean currents can affect climate by increasing temperatures over land with warm-water currents or decreasing temperature over land with cold-water currents.

The land cover of a region is another factor that controls the climate. For example, is the region covered by land or water? Land and water masses absorb energy at different rates. Also, the presence of large landforms, such as mountain ranges, can block the movement of air masses. All of these factors control the climate of a region.

Importance of Climate

Climate is an abiotic factor that determines where species can survive. A biome is an area in which the climate typically determines the plant community, which in turn supports the animal community. Similar biomes are found in different parts of the world where the climate is similar. Species are adapted to a specific biome and a specific climate. A change in climate, such as global warming, impacts all organisms on Earth. Organisms will either adapt to the new conditions, immigrate to a new habitat if available, or die if the changes are severe.

Under normal circumstances, climate controls access to food, fresh water, and energy. Humans are adapted to specific climates, though humans are capable of using technology to live in climates we would not normally be adapted to. Climate and weather-related natural disasters, such as hurricanes or wildfires, cause billions of dollars in damage each year.

What Affects Earth's Climate?

Fill in the blank.

1. Latitudes near the _____ receive the most direct solar energy.

2. _____ is water that falls from the atmosphere and reaches Earth's surface.

3. As altitude increases, temperature _____.

4. A(n) _____ is an area in which the climate typically determines the plant community.

5. _____ is the study of climates, including past, present, and future climates.

6. _____ is the movement of air caused by difference in air pressure.

7. Climate is a(n) _____ factor that determines where species can survive.

8. **Main Idea** What is climate?

_____

_____

_____

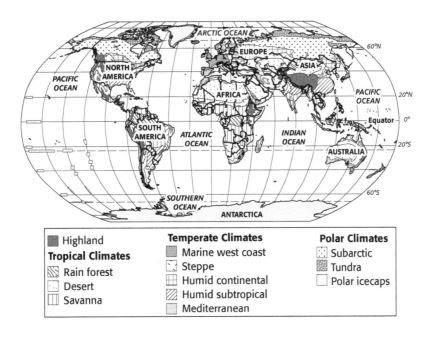

71

9. **Vocabulary** Write a paragraph describing atmospheric conditions using the terms *precipitation, wind*, and *convection current*.

_____

_____

_____

10. **Reading Skill: Main Idea and Details** Why is climate important to humans?

_____

_____

_____

11. **Critical Thinking: Evaluate** Describe the role that climate plays in determining the types and numbers of organisms that live in an area.

_____

_____

_____

12. **Inquiry Skill: Infer** How would winds be affected if Earth's surface was the same temperature everywhere? Explain.

_____

_____

_____

13. **Test Prep** The sun's energy creates pressure differences in Earth's atmosphere. As high-pressure areas are created around the poles, cold polar air will flow toward

   A the equator.

   B the North Pole.

   C the South Pole.

   D the atmosphere.

What Is the Relationship Between Earth and Living Things?

Earth System

Earth consists of rock, air, water, and living things that all interact with one another. Scientists divide this system into four parts: the geosphere (rock), the atmosphere (air), the hydrosphere (water), and the biosphere (living things).

The solid part of Earth that consists of all rock, as well as the soils and loose rocks on Earth's surface, makes up the geosphere. Most of the geosphere is located in Earth's interior, within its liquid mantle and dense core. The outermost layer of Earth, its crust, includes its surface features. Forces within the geosphere affect living and nonliving things. Tectonic plates move slowly, changing the shape of Earth's continents. Molten rock from Earth's interior flows over the surface of the planet, and violent eruptions blow the tops off volcanoes. Earthquakes shake the ground and topple natural and artificial structures.

The atmosphere is the mixture of gases that make up the air we breathe. Nearly all of these gases are found in the first 30 km above Earth's surface. Earth's atmosphere changes constantly as these gases are added and removed. For example, animals remove oxygen from the atmosphere when they breathe in and add carbon dioxide when they breathe out. Plants take in carbon dioxide and add oxygen to the atmosphere when they produce food. Gases can also be added when a volcano erupts. The atmosphere insulates Earth's surface. This insulation slows the rate at which Earth's surface loses heat. The atmosphere keeps Earth at temperatures at which living things can survive. It also is the source of weather that alters Earth's surface and affects its inhabitants.

The hydrosphere is all of the water on or near the Earth's surface. Mostly in the oceans, water is also in the atmosphere, on land, and in the soil. The hydrosphere interacts with the atmosphere and geosphere, as well as with living things. The continuous movement of water into the air, onto land, and then back to water sources is known as the water cycle. Hurricanes and other storms batter beaches and change coastlines. Erosion by rivers and oceans produces changes on Earth's surface and gives rise to a variety of landforms.

The biosphere is made up of all the parts of the geosphere, the atmosphere, and the hydrosphere where life can exist. It is a thin layer at Earth's surface that extends from about 9 km above the Earth's surface down to the bottom of the ocean. The biosphere is located near Earth's surface because most of the sunlight is available near the surface. Plants and algae on land and in the ocean need sunlight to produce their food, and almost every other organism gets its food from plants and algae.

Development of Earth's Atmosphere

Earth's original atmosphere consisted primarily of hydrogen and helium. However, Earth's gravity was too weak to hold these light gases. The sun heated the gases enough so that they escaped Earth's gravity. As time passed and Earth's surface formed, frequent volcanic eruptions released large amounts of water vapor, carbon dioxide, nitrogen, methane, sulfur dioxide, and ammonia. This process formed a new atmosphere. The gases reacted with radiation from the sun. Ammonia and some of the water vapor in the atmosphere broke down. Most of the hydrogen that was released during this breakdown escaped into space. Some of the remaining oxygen formed ozone, a molecule that contains three oxygen atoms. The ozone collected in the stratosphere and shielded Earth's surface from harmful ultraviolet radiation from the sun.

Organisms that could survive in this atmosphere evolved. Some of these organisms, such as cyanobacteria, used carbon dioxide during photosynthesis. Oxygen, a byproduct of photosynthesis, was released. The amount of oxygen in the atmosphere slowly increased, as did the variety of life on Earth. Today, this cycling of gases still continues. During photosynthesis, organisms take in carbon dioxide from the air and add oxygen to the air. During respiration, organisms take in oxygen and add carbon dioxide to the air.

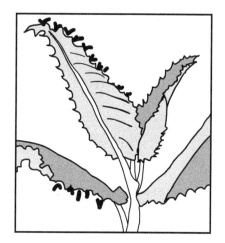

Kalanchoe plants produce **plantlets** along the edges of their leaves. The plantlets eventually fall off and root in the soil to grow their own.

Origins of Life: The Primordial Soup Model

Scientists who study the origins of life think that the path to the development of living things began when molecules of nonliving matter reacted chemically during the first billion years of Earth's history. These chemical reactions produced many different simple, organic molecules. Energized by the sun and volcanic heat, these simple, organic molecules formed more complex molecules that eventually became the building blocks of the first cells.

In the 1920s, the Russian scientist A. I. Oparin and the British scientist J. B. S. Haldane both suggested that early Earth's oceans contained large amounts of organic molecules. This hypothesis became known as the primordial soup model. Earth's vast oceans were thought to be filled with many different organic molecules. Oparin and Haldane hypothesized that these molecules formed spontaneously in chemical reactions activated by energy from solar radiation, volcanic eruptions, and lightning.

In 1953, the primordial soup model was tested by American scientists Stanley Miller and Harold Urey. Miller placed the gases that he and Urey proposed had existed on early Earth into a device made up of glass tubes and vessels. To simulate lightning, he provided electrical sparks. After a few days, Miller found a complex collection of organic molecules, including some of life's basic building blocks: amino acids, fatty acids, and other hydrocarbons. These results support the hypothesis that some basic chemicals of life could have formed spontaneously under conditions like those in the experiment. Scientists have reevaluated the Miller-Urey experiment in light of the fact that we now know that four billion years ago, Earth did not have a protective layer of ozone gas, O^3. Without ozone, ultraviolet radiation would have destroyed any ammonia and methane present in the atmosphere.

Origins of Life: The Bubble Model

In 1986, the geophysicist Louis Lerman suggested that the key processes that formed the chemicals needed for life took place within bubbles beneath the ocean's surface. In this bubble model, he proposed that ammonia, methane, and other gases resulting from the numerous eruptions of undersea volcanoes were trapped in underwater bubbles. Inside the bubbles, these gases might have been protected from damaging ultraviolet radiation and could have undergone chemical reactions. Eventually, the bubbles rose to the surface and burst, releasing simple organic molecules into the air. In the air, the simple organic molecules were exposed to ultraviolet radiation and lightning, which provided energy for further reactions. The more complex organic molecules that formed fell into the ocean with rain, starting another cycle.

What Is the Relationship Between Earth and Living Things?

Fill in the blank.

1. During photosynthesis, organisms take in _____ from the air and add

   _____ to the air.

2. _____ is a molecule that contains three oxygen atoms and protects Earth's
   surface from ultraviolet radiation from the sun.

3. Earth's original atmosphere consisted primarily of _____ and

   _____.

4. The _____ suggested that the development of complex organic molecules
   occurred within bubbles in the ocean.

5. The _____ is the mixture of gases that make up the air we breathe.

6. The _____ is all of the water on or near the Earth's surface.

7. The _____ model suggested that the development of complex organic
   molecules occurred freely within Earth's oceans.

8. **Main Idea** What is the relationship between Earth and living things?

   _____

   _____

   _____

Miller-Urey Experiment

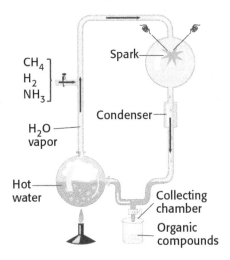

9. **Vocabulary** Write a paragraph explaining how the systems on Earth interact using the terms *geosphere*, *atmosphere*, *hydrosphere*, and *biosphere*.

_____

_____

_____

10. **Reading Skill: Main Idea and Details** What important role did bubbles play according to the bubble model?

_____

_____

_____

_____

11. **Critical Thinking: Compare** Two models of the origin of life on Earth are the primordial soup model and the bubble model. What do these two models of how life on Earth began have in common?

_____

_____

_____

12. **Inquiry Skill: Explain** How did photosynthesizing organisms contribute to the composition of Earth's atmosphere?

_____

_____

_____

13. **Test Prep** What was one effect of the development of the ozone layer on life on Earth?

   A The ozone layer provided additional oxygen for large land animals.

   B The ozone layer provided protection from ultraviolet radiation and made it safer for life forms to live on land.

   C The ozone layer provided protection to the polar regions of Earth and promoted the development of new polar species.

   D The ozone layer helped to warm the oceans and promoted the development of new aquatic species.

What Are Natural Resources?

Natural Resource

A natural resource is any natural material that is used by humans. Examples of natural resources are water, petroleum, minerals, forests, soil, and animals. Most resources are used in products that make people's lives more comfortable. The energy we get from resources, such as gasoline and wind, ultimately come from the sun's energy.

Some natural resources can be renewed. A renewable resource can be replaced at the same rate at which it is used. Although many resources could be renewable, some are being used up before they can be renewed. Trees, for example, can be renewable. However, some forests are being cut down faster than new forests can grow to replace them. And as the forests disappear, so do their inhabitants. Furthermore, as species disappear, so do our chances to learn about them and their possible benefits.

Not all of Earth's natural resources are renewable. A nonrenewable resource forms at a rate that is much slower than the rate at which it is consumed. When these resources become scarce, humans will have to find other resources to replace them. Most of the energy we use comes from a group of natural resources called fossil fuels. A fossil fuel is a nonrenewable energy resource formed from the remains of plants and animals that lived long ago. Examples of fossil fuels include petroleum, coal, and natural gas. Once fossil fuels are used up, new supplies won't be available for thousands—or even millions—of years. In addition, obtaining and using fossil fuels has environmental consequences, such as acid rain. To continue having access to energy and to overcome pollution, we must find alternative sources of energy.

Renewable Energy

There are many sources of renewable energy that are currently being developed. It is important to note that just because an energy source is considered renewable does not mean that it has no impact on the environment.

Solar power is harvested from sunlight using solar cells. Solar power is an almost limitless source of energy, and it does not produce pollution. However, solar power is currently expensive to use for large-scale energy production and it is only practical in sunny areas.

Water power, or hydropower, is the power harvested from running or falling water. Hydropower is a renewable resource that does not produce air pollution. Hydropower often requires dams, which can disrupt a river's ecosystem. Also, hydropower is available only where there are rivers.

Geothermal energy is an almost limitless source of energy that originates in the interior of the earth. Power plants to harvest geothermal energy require little land. However, geothermal energy is practical only in areas near hot spots, and geothermal power produces wastewater, which can damage soil.

Biomass is material from living or recently living organisms. Energy can be obtained from biomass by burning the biomass or by chemically converting the biomass into useable energy. The production of biomass can require large areas of farmland. However, sometimes energy can be harvested from biomass that is the by-product of other industries, such as used urban wood. The burning of biomass produces smoke and other air pollution.

Fuel cells are another way to use renewable energy. Fuel cells power automobiles by converting chemical energy into electrical energy through the reaction of hydrogen and oxygen into water. One advantage of using fuel cells as energy sources is that fuel cells do not create pollution. The only by-product of fuel cells is water. Fuel cells are also more efficient than internal combustion engines.

Sustainability

The United Nations projects that the world's population will stabilize at 9.7 billion by the year 2050. No one knows whether Earth can support its current population of more than six billion people indefinitely, much less the far larger population of the future. Already our limited supply of natural resources is becoming depleted or polluted.

Building a sustainable world is an important task facing humanity. The quality of life available to children in this new century will depend to a large extent on our success. One way to help preserve our world is through sustainable practices—practices that help support human activity without depleting natural resources. For example, sustainable agriculture is farming that remains productive and profitable through practices that help replenish the soil's nutrients, reduce erosion, and control weeds and insect pests. Through such practices, humans can support the world's population without further depleting or damaging valuable natural resources.

Reducing and Recycling

Whether the natural resources you use are renewable or nonrenewable, you should be careful of how you use them. To conserve natural resources, you should try to use them only when necessary. Another way to conserve natural resources is to recycle. Recycling is the process of reusing materials from waste or scrap. Recycling reduces the amount of natural resources that must be obtained from Earth. Recycling also conserves energy. Newspaper, aluminum cans, most plastic containers, and cardboard boxes can be recycled. Most plastic containers have a number on them. This number informs you whether the item can be recycled.

As with all natural resources, conserving energy is important. You can conserve energy by being careful to use only the resources that you need. For example, turn lights off when you are not using them. And make sure the washing machine is full before you start it. You can also ride a bike, walk, or take a bus, because these methods use fewer resources than a car does.

What Are Natural Resources?

Match each term to its correct definition.

Definitions

_____ **1.** energy harvested from running water

_____ **2.** reusing materials from waste or scrap

_____ **3.** energy harvested from sunlight

_____ **4.** natural material used by humans

_____ **5.** resource that is replaced at the same rate it is consumed

_____ **6.** resource that forms slower than the rate it is consumed

_____ **7.** energy from Earth's interior

Terms

a. natural resource

b. hydropower

c. nonrenewable re-source

d. renewable resource

e. solar power

f. recycling

g. geothermal energy

Write the answer to the question on the lines below.

8. Main Idea What are natural resources?

_____

_____

Earth Science
Core Skills Science, Grade 8

9. **Vocabulary** Write a sentence using the terms *solar power* and *hydropower*.

_____

_____

10. **Reading Skill: Compare and Contrast** Describe the difference between renewable and nonrenewable resources.

_____

_____

_____

11. **Critical Thinking: Evaluate** Describe three ways you could help conserve resources.

_____

_____

12. **Inquiry Skill: Predict** About 260,000 people are added to the world population each day, or about 180 every minute. Identify three natural resources that could become depleted or damaged as a result of the increasing human population.

_____

_____

_____

13. **Test Prep** What practice represents a sustainable practice in the fishing industry?

    A maintaining a fishery that can supply the same number of fish as are harvested each year

    B harvesting all of the fish in one area in a short period of time

    C sending fishing boats to harvest in areas where fish are not usually found in great numbers

    D overfishing of species near the bottom of the food chain in place of species at the top of the food chain

What Is Sustainability?

Natural Resources

Remember that nonrenewable resources cannot be replaced or are replaced much more slowly than they are used. Fossil fuels are the most important nonrenewable resources. Renewable resources are naturally replaced more quickly than they are used. Some renewable resources, such as solar energy and wind energy, are considered practically limitless.

Fossil fuels provide a large amount of thermal energy per unit of mass. They are relatively easy to get and transport, and they can be used to generate electricity and to make products such as plastic. However, fossil fuels are nonrenewable, they produce smog, they release substances that can cause acid precipitation, and they contribute to global warming.

Every individual on Earth uses natural resources. On average, individuals in developed countries use more resources than individuals in undeveloped countries. This includes resources such as food, water, and energy. The consumption of natural resources will continue to increase as the world population increases. One way to reduce human impact on Earth is to implement technology that can increase energy efficiency and minimize the use of natural resources.

Sustainability

Sustainability is the condition in which human society can go on indefinitely and future generations can have a standard of living as high as the present one. To live in a sustainable way, it is essential to look for new solutions to problems. For example, fresh water and energy are becoming scarce and expensive in many parts of the world. We need to develop sustainable solutions. Suppose that we developed cheap, renewable, non-polluting sources of energy. We could then make all the fresh water we needed by desalinating (removing the salt from) sea water, solving both problems. By approaching problems with sustainability in mind, each new solution builds a better world.

Sustainable Agriculture

One industry where sustainable practices can help support human activity is agriculture. Sustainable agriculture refers to farming that remains productive and profitable through practices that replenish the soil's nutrients, reduce erosion, and control weeds and insect pests. Sustainable agriculture minimizes the use of artificial fertilizer and pesticides, which reduces pollution and provides health benefits for humans and the surrounding ecosystems.

In an ecosystem, decomposers return mineral nutrients to the soil. However, when the plants are harvested and shipped away, there is a net loss of nutrients from the soil where the plants were growing. The amount of organic matter in the soil also decreases, making the soil less able to hold water and more likely to erode.

One way to protect soil is through the planting of cover crops. After harvest, farmers can plant crops such as rye, clover, or vetch instead of letting the ground lie bare. These cover crops keep the soil from compacting and washing away, and they help the soil absorb water. They also provide habitat for beneficial insects, slow the growth of weeds, and keep the ground from overheating. When cover crops are plowed under, they return nutrients to the soil.

Rotational grazing can also protect land resources. Farmers who raise cattle and sheep can divide their pastures into several grazing areas. By rotating their livestock from one area to another, they can prevent the animals from overgrazing the pasture. This allows the plants on which the animals feed to live longer and be more productive. Water quality improves as the pasture vegetation becomes denser. Animals distribute manure more evenly with rotational grazing than they do in feed lots or unmanaged pastures.

Green Building

The concept of sustainability does not apply only to agricultural practices. Sustainable technology can be implemented in many areas of society. For example, many technologies have been developed to make buildings and homes more energy efficient.

Homes and buildings are where humans spend much of their time. Homes and buildings are also where a good deal of natural resources, including energy, are invested. Energy efficient appliances and light bulbs can be installed that will decrease the amount of energy used. Toilets have been developed that use less water when they flush. Composting toilets have also been engineered that use little or no water. A living roof is a roof that has live vegetation. Living roofs provide insulation and create habitat for plants and animals, among other benefits. Solar panels and wind turbines can be installed on premise to provide a source of renewable energy for the facilities. All of this technology has been designed to make modern life on Earth more sustainable.

What Is Sustainability?

Write answers to the questions on the lines below.

1. Are fossil fuels a renewable resource or a nonrenewable resource?

   _____

2. Do individuals in developed countries use more or fewer resources than individuals in undeveloped countries?

   _____

   _____

3. Is solar energy renewable or nonrenewable?

   _____

4. Name one benefit of a living roof.

   _____

5. What is desalination?

   _____

6. What is rotational grazing?

   _____

   _____

7. Which nonrenewable resource can be used to make plastic?

   _____

8. **Main Idea** What is sustainability?

   _____

   _____

   _____

9. Vocabulary Write a paragraph explaining sustainability using the terms *renewable resource* and *nonrenewable resource*.

_____

_____

_____

10. Reading Skill: Main Idea and Details What are three benefits of cover crops?

_____

_____

_____

11. Critical Thinking: Apply What would be one benefit of living in a green home?

_____

_____

12. Inquiry Skill: Predict What could be one challenge to farmers who decided to plant cover crops?

_____

_____

_____

13. Test Prep Sustainable agriculture is farming that remains productive and profitable while still conserving natural resources. Which of the following is an example of a sustainable agricultural practice?

A preventing cattle from ever grazing on pastures

B removing all manure from pastures where cattle graze

C allowing cattle to graze over an entire pasture year round

D rotating parts of a pasture on which cattle graze throughout the year

How Does Earth's Climate Change?

Climate

A region's climate is not the same thing as the weather. Climate describes the average weather conditions of an area over a given period of time. Weather describes atmospheric events that affect a small area over a short time period. Climate is used to describe long-term weather patterns that occur on a larger scale, such as a regional or global climate.

Scientists agree that Earth's climate is steadily warming at a faster than normal rate. The burning of fossil fuels is the most probable root cause of the warming trends on Earth. Earth's climate also changes naturally through very long cycles of ice ages and interglacial periods.

Milankovitch Cycle

Changes in the shape of Earth's orbit, the tilt of its axis, and the wobble of Earth on its axis can lead to climate changes. Each change of motion has a different effect on climate. These changes, called Milankovitch cycles, occur in cycles of 21,000 to 100,000 years.

Variations in the shape of Earth's orbit, from elliptical to circular, affect Earth's distance from the sun. Earth's distance from the sun affects the temperature of Earth and therefore affects the climate. Earth's energy from the sun varies more when Earth's orbit is elongated than when it is circular.

Decreasing the tilt of Earth's axis decreases temperature differences between seasons. The tilt of Earth's axis varies between 22.2° and 24.5°. The greater the tilt of the angle, the more solar energy the poles receive.

The wobble of Earth on its axis changes the direction of Earth's tilt. It affects the amount of solar radiation that reaches different parts of Earth's surface at different times of the year. Changes in the wobble of Earth's axis can reverse seasons.

Ice Age

Changes in Milankovitch cycles can lead to periods of glaciation, commonly called ice ages. The earliest known ice age began about 800 million years ago. The most recent ice age began about 4 million years ago. A glacier is a large body of ice, such as an ice sheet. The last advance of this ice age's massive ice sheets reached its peak about 18,000 years ago. Ice ages probably begin with a long, slow decrease in Earth's average temperatures. A drop in average global temperature of only about 5°C may be enough to start an ice age.

Continental glaciers advance and retreat several times during an ice age. The ice sheets advance during colder periods and retreat during warmer periods. A period of cooler climate that is characterized by the advancement of glaciers is called a glacial period.

A period of warmer climate that is characterized by the retreat of glaciers is called an interglacial period. Currently, Earth is in an interglacial period of the most recent ice age.

Effects of Climate Change

During the last glacial period, which ended about 15,000 years ago, some of the water that is now in the ocean existed as continental ice sheets. Scientists estimate that the ice sheets held about 70 million cubic kilometers of ice. Currently, the ice sheets in Antarctica and Greenland hold only about 25 million cubic kilometers of ice.

During the last glacial period, the water that made up the additional 45 million cubic kilometers of ice is thought to have come from the oceans. As a result, sea level was as much as 140 meters (m) lower during the last glacial period than it is today. Since the last glacial period, the ice sheets have been melting and sea level has been rising at a rate of about 1 millimeter (mm) per year. If, in the distant future, the polar ice caps were to melt completely, the oceans would rise about 60 m and submerge low-lying coastal regions. The locations of many large cities, such as New York, Los Angeles, Miami, and Houston, would be submerged.

glacier

How Does Earth's Climate Change?

Write answers to the questions on the lines below.

1. When did the last ice age reach its peak?

_____

2. What is currently happening to the sea level?

_____

_____

3. What is climate?

_____

_____

4. How do changes in the wobble of Earth on its axis affect climate?

_____

_____

5. What is a glacier?

_____

6. What is a glacial period?

_____

_____

7. Earth is currently in what kind of period?

_____

8. **Main Idea** What is a Milankovitch cycle?

_____

_____

_____

_____

9. Vocabulary Write a paragraph comparing an *ice age* and an *interglacial period*.

_____

_____

_____

10. Reading Skill: Cause and Effect How do changes in the tilt of Earth's axis affect climate?

_____

_____

11. Critical Thinking: Infer Why is the length of Milankovitch cycles important when discussing current global climate change?

_____

_____

_____

12. Inquiry Skill: Predict Global warming, or an increase in Earth's surface temperatures, can cause changes in sea level. Why is this a concern?

_____

_____

_____

_____

13. Test Prep When would Earth receive the most variation in energy from the sun?

    A when its orbit is circular

    B when its orbit is elongated

    C when its axis is at an angle of 22.2°

    D when its axis is at an angle of 24.5°

What Are States of Matter?

Matter is anything that has mass and takes up space. The three most common states of matter are solid, liquid, and gas. States of matter are defined based on the energy and motion of the particles that make up a substance. The kinetic-molecular theory is based on the idea that particles of matter are always in motion. The theory can be used to explain the properties of solids, liquids, and gases in terms of the energy of particles and the forces that act between them.

Gases

Gases do not have a definite shape or a definite volume. They completely fill any container in which they are enclosed, and they take its shape. A gas transferred from a one-liter vessel to a two-liter vessel will quickly expand to fill the entire two-liter volume.

Gas particles move rapidly in all directions without significant attraction between them, so gas particles glide easily past one another. The density of a gaseous substance at atmospheric pressure is about 1/1000 the density of the same substance in the liquid or solid state because the particles are so much farther apart. The volume of a given sample of a gas can be greatly decreased by increasing the pressure, or forcing the particles closer together.

Gases spread out and mix with one another, even without being stirred, due to the random and continuous motion of atoms or molecules. This mixing process is called diffusion.

Liquids

A liquid has a definite volume and takes the shape of its container. As in a gas, particles in a liquid are in constant motion, but the particles in a liquid are closer together than the particles in a gas. Attractive forces between particles in a liquid are more effective than those between particles in a gas. This attraction between liquid particles is caused by intermolecular forces.

Liquids are more ordered than gases because of the stronger intermolecular forces and the lower mobility of the liquid particles. The particles are not bound together in fixed positions, so they move about constantly. Liquids are much denser than gases because of the close arrangement of liquid particles. Most substances are only slightly less dense in a liquid state than in a solid state. Water is one of the few substances that becomes less dense when it solidifies.

Liquids are much less compressible than gases because liquid particles are more closely packed together. The constant random motion of particles causes diffusion in liquids, as it does in gases, but at a much slower rate.

Solids

The particles of a solid are more closely packed than those of a gas. They are usually more closely packed than those of a liquid, as well. Intermolecular forces exert stronger effects in solids than in the corresponding liquids or gases. These attractive forces tend to hold the particles of a solid in relatively fixed positions, with only vibrational movement around fixed points. Because the motions of the particles are restricted in this way, solids are more ordered than liquids and are much more ordered than gases. Unlike liquids and gases, solids can maintain a definite shape without a container. Solids have definite volume because their particles are packed closely together. For practical purposes, solids can be considered incompressible.

Change of State

If energy is added to a substance, its particles move faster. If energy is removed, the substance's particles move slower. For instance, the particles in steam have more energy than the particles in liquid water. A transfer of energy known as heat causes the temperature of a substance to change. If enough energy is added or removed, the substance will change state.

When water vapor in the air becomes a liquid, energy is released from the water to its surroundings. This is an example of condensation, which is the change of state from a gas to a liquid. For a gas to become a liquid, large numbers of gas particles clump together. Energy is released from the gas, and the particles slow down. Energy is also released during freezing, which is the change of state from a liquid to a solid. For a liquid to freeze, the attractions between the particles must overcome their motion.

When a solid changes to a liquid, energy is absorbed. The phase change from a solid to a liquid is called melting. Energy is also absorbed when a liquid changes to a gas. This process is known as vaporization.

Temperature is constant during changes of state. When a substance loses or gains energy, either its temperature changes or its state changes. But the temperature of a substance does not change during a change of state. For example, if you add energy to ice at 0°C, the temperature will not rise until all of the ice has melted.

A heating curve, such as the graph to the right, shows the changes that a substance undergoes when heat is added to or removed from the substance. Any change in temperature and any change in state, or phase change, involves a change in energy. The energy absorbed during a phase change helps the particles overcome some of the attractions between them and increases their freedom of motion. But because the average kinetic energy of the particles does not change, there is no change in temperature during a phase change.

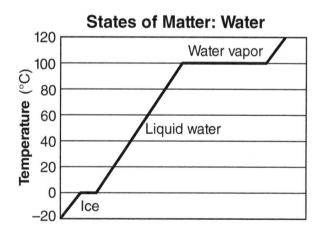

90

Physical Science
Core Skills Science, Grade 8

What Are States of Matter?

Match each term to its correct definition.

Definitions

_____ 1. change of state from a solid to a liquid, energy is absorbed

_____ 2. state of matter with a definite volume that takes the shape of its container

_____ 3. mixing of a substance due to random and continuous movement of particles

_____ 4. change of state from a gas to a liquid, energy is released

_____ 5. state of matter with definite shape and volume

_____ 6. change of state from a liquid to a solid, energy is released

_____ 7. state of matter without a definite shape or volume

_____ 8. change of state from a liquid to a gas, energy is absorbed

Terms

a. solid

b. liquid

c. gas

d. diffusion

e. condensation

f. vaporization

g. melting

h. freezing

9. **Main Idea** What are states of matter?

_____

_____

_____

10. Vocabulary Write a paragraph that describes particle motion using the terms *solid*, *liquid*, and *gas*.

_____

_____

_____

11. Reading Skill: Sequence Describe, in order, what changes in energy would have to occur for a substance to change from a liquid to a gas and then back into a liquid.

_____

_____

_____

12. Critical Thinking: Analyze In which state of matter are the bonds between particles strongest? Explain.

_____

_____

_____

13. Inquiry Skill: Compare What would happen to liquid water if energy is removed? What about if energy is added? What processes do these changes represent?

_____

_____

_____

_____

14. Test Prep Look at the graph to the right.

What is happening in the range where the line is horizontal?

A Particles are no longer locked in position.

B Particles are rearranging from a solid into a liquid.

C Particles are rearranging from a liquid into a solid.

D Particles have acquired enough energy to slide past one another.

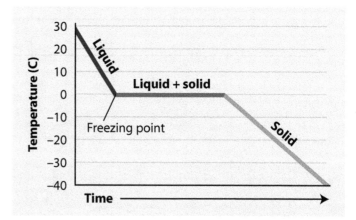

Physical Science
Core Skills Science, Grade 8

How Are Reference Points Used to Measure Motion?

Motion and Reference Points

When an object changes position over time relative to a reference point, the object is in motion. The movement of an object is always measured by comparing its position to that of a stationary reference point. To fully describe the motion of an object, its position, speed, and direction need to be considered.

Earth's surface is a common reference point for determining motion; however, anything near a moving object can be used as a frame of reference for describing motion. The chalkboard in a classroom can be a frame of reference for anything in the room. A tree outside can be a frame of reference for a bird flying by. Motion can sometimes be described by using more than one frame of reference. For example, a person sitting on a bus is not moving in relation to the seats in the bus or in relation to another passenger, but the person is moving in relation to the ground or in relation to a car traveling in the opposite direction.

Speed

Motion is the change of position of an object relative to a reference point. A reference point is an object that appears to stay in place. The object's speed is the rate at which its distance is changing compared to the reference point. So, speed is a measure of the rate of change of an object's position.

If an object is moving at a constant rate, its speed can be determined by dividing the distance over which it moves by the time needed to move that distance. The speedometer of a car shows how fast the car is moving at any particular time. When you calculate the speed of an object, its direction does not matter, only the distance and the time.

Speed can be determined from a graph of motion. Speed is the slope of the line on the graph. In the Distance vs. Time graph below, the speed of object *a* can be calculated by dividing change in distance by time, or 43 m ÷ 40 s = 1.075 m/s. For object *b*, the distance did not change, so the speed is 0 m/s.

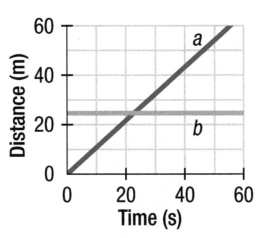

Distance vs. Time

© Houghton Mifflin Harcourt Publishing Company

Physical Science
Core Skills Science, Grade 8

Velocity

Velocity is a measure of displacement, which is determined by the speed and direction of motion. So, velocity is the speed of an object in a particular direction. Be careful not to confuse the terms *speed* and *velocity*. They do not have the same meaning. Using SI units (the International System of Units), velocity is measured in meters per second (m/s).

Velocity must include a reference direction, which means that velocity is always measured relative to a reference point. If you say that an airplane's velocity is 600 km/h, you would not be correct. However, you could say that the plane's velocity is 600 km/h south, using Earth's surface as a reference. You can think of velocity as the rate of change of an object's position in a particular direction.

An object's velocity is constant only if its speed and direction do not change. Therefore, constant velocity is always motion along a straight line. An object's velocity changes if either its speed or direction changes.

Acceleration

Acceleration is the rate at which velocity changes. So, acceleration is the change in velocity over time. If velocity is in a constant direction, the acceleration can be determined by the change in speed or velocity divided by time. In the Velocity vs. Time graph below, the acceleration of object c can be calculated by dividing change in velocity by time: 43 m/s ÷ 40 s = 1.075 m/s². For object d, the velocity did not change, so the acceleration is 0 m/s².

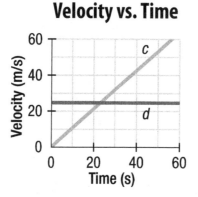

Velocity changes if speed changes, if direction changes, or if both change. So, an object accelerates if its speed, its direction, or both change. Acceleration depends not only on how much velocity changes, but also on how fast velocity changes. The faster the velocity changes, the greater the acceleration. Like velocity, acceleration must be measured relative to a reference point.

When a bus driver steps on the gas pedal, the bus will experience acceleration because its speed is increasing. The bus driver can also change the velocity of the bus by turning. In this situation, the bus might not change its speed, but its direction will be different, so it is accelerating. Because acceleration is the change in velocity over time, the units for acceleration look like the units for velocity (m/s) divided by time (s). Thus, the most common units of acceleration are meters per second per second, or (m/s)/s. This unit is often written as m/s².

How Are Reference Points Used to Measure Motion?

Fill in the blank.

1. _____ is the rate at which velocity changes.

2. Speed is the _____ of the line on a graph of motion.

3. _____ is the change of position of an object relative to a reference point.

4. Velocity is the _____ of an object in a particular direction.

5. Using SI units, velocity is measured in _____.

6. Constant velocity is always motion along a(n) _____ line.

7. The most common units for acceleration are _____.

8. **Main Idea** How are reference points used to measure motion?

_____

_____

_____

9. **Vocabulary** Write a sentence using the terms *acceleration*, *velocity*, and *speed*.

_____

_____

_____

10. **Reading Skill: Main Idea and Details** How are speed and reference points related?

_____

_____

11. **Critical Thinking: Apply** What is the acceleration of a stationary object? Explain your answer.

_____

_____

_____

12. **Inquiry Skill: Infer** How can two objects have the same speeds but different velocities?

_____

_____

13. **Test Prep** A boy in a canoe paddles upriver at a speed of 1.4 m/s relative to the water. The water flows downriver at a speed of 1.4 m/s relative to the riverbed. How fast does the boy's canoe appear to move when viewed by an observer standing on the riverbank?

   A 0 m/s

   B 1.4 m/s up the river

   C 1.4 m/s down the river

   D 2.8 m/s up the river

What Is Gravity?

Describing Gravity

Johannes Kepler used the observations of Tycho Brahe to discover three basic laws that describe the motion of planets in their orbits around the sun. Later, Sir Isaac Newton explained the motions of the planets of the solar system at the same time that he described the force of gravity. Newton didn't understand why gravity worked or what caused it. Even today, scientists do not fully understand gravity. But Newton combined the work of earlier scientists and used mathematics to explain the effects of gravity. Newton was able to show that Kepler's laws of planetary motion could be derived from three laws of motion and the assumption that a force, "gravity," drew all bodies with mass towards each other.

Because a planet does not follow a straight path, an outside force must cause the orbit to curve. Newton discovered that this force is gravity, and he realized that this attractive force exists between any two objects in the universe. The gravitational pull of the sun keeps objects in orbit around the sun. While gravity pulls an object toward the sun, inertia keeps the object moving forward in a straight line. The sum of these two motions forms the ellipse of a stable orbit.

Newton reasoned that an object falls toward Earth because Earth and the object are attracted to each other by gravity. He discovered that this attraction depends on the masses of the objects and the distance between the objects. Both Earth and the moon are attracted to each other. Although it may seem as if Earth does not orbit the moon, Earth and the moon actually orbit each other.

Why doesn't the moon come crashing into Earth? The answer has to do with the moon's inertia. Inertia is an object's resistance to a change in speed or direction until an outside force acts on the object. In space, there isn't any air to cause resistance and slow down the moving moon. Therefore, the moon continues to move, but gravity keeps the moon in its orbit. Gravity keeps the moon from flying off in a straight path. This principle holds true for all bodies in orbit, including Earth and other planets in our solar system as they orbit the sun.

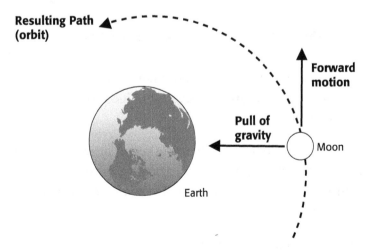

Gravity, Mass, and Weight

Gravity is one of the four fundamental forces of nature. Gravitational forces are relatively weak, but they can act over great distances.

All matter has mass. The mass of an object is a measure of the amount of matter it contains, so mass is a constant characteristic of a particular object. Gravity is a result of mass. Therefore, all matter is affected by gravity. That is, all objects experience an attraction toward all other objects. This gravitational force pulls objects toward each other.

Weight is a measure of the force of gravity on the object, which is proportional to the mass. Therefore, weight is a function of the masses of the object and the larger object to which it is attracted, so weight can vary. For example, Earth is more massive than the moon, so a person would not weigh as much on the moon as on Earth. Weight is equal to the mass of an object times the acceleration of gravity. The SI unit for weight is the newton, named for Isaac Newton. A newton is equal to 1 kilogram-meter per second squared ($kg \cdot m/s^2$).

Law of Universal Gravitation

According to the Law of Universal Gravitation, all objects in the universe attract each other through gravitational force. The size of the force depends on the masses of the objects and the distance between the objects. The gravitational force is stronger when the masses are greater or when the objects are closer together.

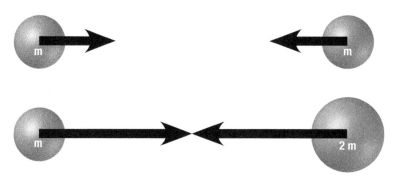

Relationship between gravitational attraction and distance

This description of gravity is considered to be a scientific law because it is a description of observations that are always true. This is not a theory of gravity because it does not explain why the attraction between objects is related to mass and distance.

Gravity is a force of attraction between objects. When you see or hear the word *weight*, it usually refers to Earth's gravitational force on an object. But weight can also be a measure of the gravitational force exerted on objects by the moon or other planets. Weight is related to mass, but they are not the same. Weight changes when gravitational force changes.

Mass is the amount of matter in an object. An object's mass does not change. Imagine that an object is moved to a place that has a greater gravitational force—such as the planet Jupiter. The object's weight will increase, but its mass will remain the same.

What Is Gravity?

Write answers to the questions on the lines below.

1. What force binds galaxies together?

   _____

2. What is the SI unit for weight?

   _____

3. Why is the Law of Universal Gravitation not a theory?

   _____

   _____

4. Gravitational force is greater on Jupiter than it is on Earth. Will an astronaut weigh more on Jupiter or on Earth?

   _____

5. What is mass?

   _____

6. What is inertia?

   _____

   _____

7. What keeps the planets in orbit around the sun?

   _____

   _____

8. **Main Idea** Correctly state the Law of Universal Gravitation.

   _____

   _____

   _____

   _____

Physical Science
Core Skills Science, Grade 8

9. Vocabulary Explain the difference between *mass* and *weight*.

_____

_____

_____

10. Reading Skill: Cause and Effect What two factors does the force of gravity between two objects depend on?

_____

_____

_____

11. Critical Thinking: Analyze Why don't you notice the gravitational pull of your body towards a pencil?

_____

_____

12. Inquiry Skill: Use Numbers Free-fall acceleration on the moon is equal to 1.6 m/s^2. What would be the weight in newtons (N) of a 75 kg astronaut on the moon?

_____

_____

_____

13. Test Prep Which of the following would increase the gravitational attraction between two objects?

    A increase the distance between them

    B increase their speed relative to each other

    C decrease the distance between them

    D decrease the mass of the smaller object

What Is Thermal Energy?

Kinetic Energy

According to kinetic theory, all matter is made of particles—atoms and molecules—that are constantly in motion. Because they are in motion, all particles of matter have kinetic energy. Temperature is a measure of average kinetic energy, or thermal energy. Thermal energy is the energy of motion of the particles of a substance. Particles of matter are constantly moving, but they do not all move at the same speed. As a result, some particles have more kinetic energy than others have. When you measure an object's temperature, you measure the average kinetic energy of the particles in the object. The more kinetic energy the particles of an object have, the higher the temperature of the object is.

Thermal Energy and States of Matter

Thermal energy is all of the kinetic energy caused by the random motion of the particles that make up an object. Thermal energy depends on the number of particles. Water, in the form of steam, has a higher temperature than water in a lake does. But the lake has more thermal energy because the lake has more water particles.

The energy of a substance also depends on the state of matter of a substance. Remember that the three states of matter are solid, liquid, and gas. Particles in these states of matter have different levels of energy. Particles in a gas have the most energy. Gases do not have a definite shape or volume. Instead, gases fill and take the shape of any container they fill. Gas particles are generally far apart, though they can be condensed by applying pressure. Particles in a liquid have less energy than particles in a gas, but more energy than particles in a solid. Liquids have a definite volume, but not a definite shape. This means they will take the shape of a container. Liquid particles are closer together and more tightly bound than gas particles. Finally, particles in a solid have the least amount of energy. Solids have a definite volume and a definite shape. The particles in a solid are densely packed and arranged in an orderly fashion.

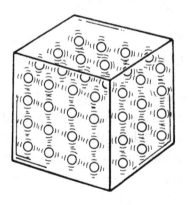

Measuring Temperature

Temperature is measured with a thermometer. To measure temperature, we use a simple physical property of substances: most substances expand when their temperatures increase. Thermometers use the expansion of liquids such as mercury or colored alcohol to measure temperature. These liquids expand as their temperature increases and contract as their temperature falls. As the temperature rises, the particles in the liquid inside a thermometer gain kinetic energy and move faster. With this increased motion, the particles in the liquid move farther apart. So, the liquid expands and rises up the narrow tube. Two objects are in thermal equilibrium if they are the same temperature.

There are three temperature scales with which you may be familiar. The Fahrenheit scale was invented in the 1700s by Daniel Fahrenheit. The Fahrenheit scale was used in English-speaking countries until the 1960s, when many countries converted to the metric system. This conversion included a switch to the Celsius scale, once known as the centigrade scale. The Fahrenheit scale is still commonly used in the United States. Water's freezing point on the Fahrenheit scale is 32°F, and its boiling point is 212°F. The freezing point of water on the Celsius scale is 0°C, and the boiling point of water is 100°C. The Kelvin scale was developed as an absolute scale. The Kelvin scale sets absolute zero at 0K, the freezing point of water at 273.15K, and the boiling point at 373.15K. The Kelvin scale is used by the scientific community. The SI unit for temperature is the kelvin (K), though everyday temperature readings in the United States are usually given in degrees Fahrenheit.

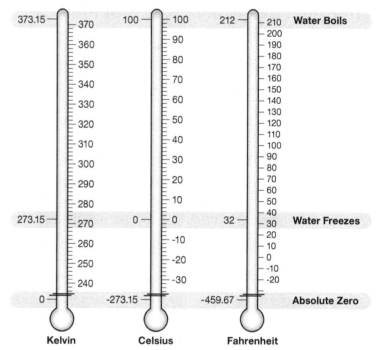

Specific Heat

The specific heat capacity of a substance is defined as the energy required to change the temperature of 1 kilogram (kg) of that substance by 1°C. Every substance has a unique specific heat capacity. This value tells you how much the temperature of a given mass of that substance will increase or decrease, based on how much energy is added or removed as heat. Pressure is a measure of how much force is applied over a given area. But what is providing this force? In kinetic theory, gas particles are likened to a collection of billiard balls that constantly collide with one another. This simple model is successful in explaining many of the macroscopic properties of a gas. For instance, as these particles strike a wall of a container, they transfer some of their momentum during the collision. The rate of transfer of momentum to the container wall is equal to the force exerted by the gas on the container wall.

What Is Thermal Energy?

Fill in the blank.

1. Thermal energy is a type of _____ energy.

2. Temperature is measured with a(n) _____.

3. Water's freezing point on the _____ scale is 32°F.

4. _____ is a measure of how much force is applied over a given area.

5. The _____ capacity of a substance is defined as the energy required to change the temperature of 1 kg of that substance by 1°C.

6. The SI unit for temperature is the _____.

7. The more kinetic energy the particles of an object have, the _____ the temperature of the object is.

8. **Main Idea** What is thermal energy?

_____

_____

_____

9. **Vocabulary** Write a paragraph explaining how temperature is measured using the terms *thermal energy*, *thermometer*, and *temperature*.

_____

_____

_____

10. **Reading Skill: Sequence** List the states of matter in order from the state that contains particles with the most energy to the state that contains particles with the least energy.

_____

_____

11. **Critical Thinking: Infer** Why is there more than one temperature scale?

_____

_____

_____

12. **Inquiry Skill: Analyze** Study the Kelvin scale and the Celsius scale. What is the relationship between the intervals on the Celsius scale and the Kelvin scale?

_____

_____

_____

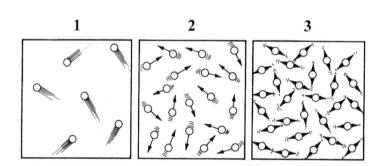

13. **Test Prep** The figures above were used to illustrate the arrangement of particles in three different states of matter. What physical state is illustrated by substance number 2?

A gas

B liquid

C plasma

D solid

How Is Energy Transferred?

Heat

Heat is the transfer of thermal energy from one object to another. Heat flows by convection, conduction, or radiation. It always flows from an object at a higher temperature to an object at a lower temperature unless work is done on the system.

Convection

Convection is the transfer of thermal energy by the movement of a liquid or a gas. When you boil water in a pot, the water moves in circular patterns because of convection. The water at the bottom of a pot on a stove burner gets hot because it is touching the pot. As it heats, the water becomes less dense. The warmer water rises through the denser, cooler water above it. At the surface, the warm water begins to cool and become denser. The cooler water then sinks back to the bottom. It is heated again, and the cycle begins again.

Convection occurs in many of Earth's systems, including the geosphere and the atmosphere. When rock is heated, it expands, becomes less dense, and tends to rise to the surface of Earth. As the rock gets near the surface, it cools, becomes denser, and tends to sink. This process forms a convection current. Convection currents cause the slow movement of tectonic plates in the lithosphere.

Convection currents also form in the atmosphere. Large masses of air move through the atmosphere by convection due to differences in pressure. Uneven heating of Earth by the sun's energy creates these differences in air pressure.

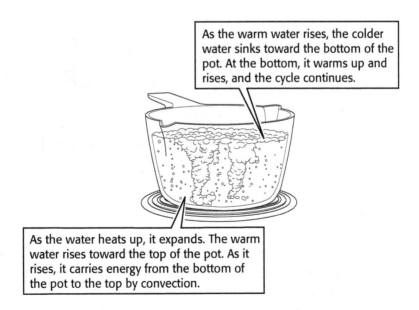

As the warm water rises, the colder water sinks toward the bottom of the pot. At the bottom, it warms up and rises, and the cycle continues.

As the water heats up, it expands. The warm water rises toward the top of the pot. As it rises, it carries energy from the bottom of the pot to the top by convection.

Conduction

Thermal conduction is the transfer of thermal energy from one substance (such as the soup in the illustration below) to another (the spoon) through direct contact. When objects touch each other, their particles collide. When particles collide, particles with higher kinetic energy transfer energy to those with lower kinetic energy. This transfer makes some particles slow down and other particles speed up until all particles have the same average kinetic energy.

The hot soup touches the spoon. Heat moves from the soup into the spoon by conduction.

The heat moves through the spoon by conduction. Heat is transferred from particle to particle in the spoon.

Radiation

A third way thermal energy is transferred is radiation (from the sun to Earth in the illustration below). Radiation is the transfer of energy by electromagnetic waves, including visible light and infrared radiation. Unlike conduction and convection, radiation can involve either an energy transfer through matter or an energy transfer through the vacuum of empty space.

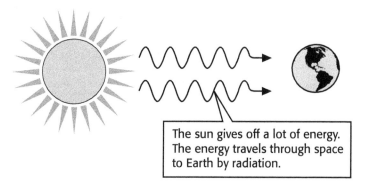

The sun gives off a lot of energy. The energy travels through space to Earth by radiation.

Energy Transfer from the Sun

The sun is the source of most energy on Earth. Energy is transferred from the sun to Earth through the process of radiation. About 35% of incoming solar radiation is reflected back into space by Earth's atmosphere and surface. About 65% is absorbed by Earth's atmosphere and surface. This thermal energy is re-reflected and heats the atmosphere by the processes of conduction and convection. Conduction occurs when Earth's surface transfers heat to that part of the atmosphere directly above it. Convection occurs when energy is transferred by the flow of gases in the atmosphere.

How Is Energy Transferred?

Fill in the blank.

1. Energy is carried from the sun to Earth by _____.

2. A spoon in a bowl of hot soup becomes warmer through _____.

3. _____ is the transfer of thermal energy from one object to another.

4. Convection _____ cause the slow movement of tectonic plates.

5. Heat usually flows from an object at a(n) _____ temperature to an object at a

   _____ temperature.

6. _____ is the transfer of energy through the movement of a liquid or a solid.

Stove burner

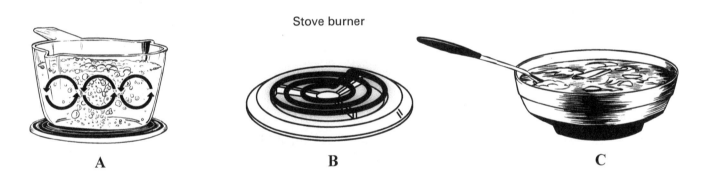

| A | B | C |

7. Which image above shows convection?

   _____

8. **Main Idea** Compare and contrast how energy is transferred through convection, conduction,
   and radiation.

   _____

   _____

   _____

   _____

9. **Vocabulary** Describe how energy is transferred to Earth from the sun using the terms *radiation, convection*, and *conduction*.

_____

_____

_____

10. **Reading Skill: Main Idea and Details** Name two locations on Earth where convection currents occur.

_____

_____

_____

11. **Critical Thinking: Infer** Just beneath the sun's visible surface, called the photosphere, is a zone where energy is transported by the rising of hot gas and the falling of cool gas. What heat transfer process is occurring in this zone? Explain your answer.

_____

_____

12. **Inquiry Skill: Apply** A spatula is sitting in water of 80°C. There is no transfer of heat energy occurring between the spatula and the water. At what temperature in °C is the spatula? Explain your answer.

_____

_____

13. **Test Prep** Two objects at different temperatures are in contact. Which of the following happens to their thermal energies?

   A Their thermal energies remain the same.

   B Thermal energy passes from the cooler object to the warmer object.

   C Thermal energy passes from the warmer object to the cooler object.

   D Thermal energy passes back and forth equally between the two objects.

How Are Energy and Forces Related?

Energy

Energy exists throughout the universe in many different forms. Energy can be broadly defined as the ability to do work. The SI unit of work is the joule, which represents the energy expended, or the amount of work done, when a force of 1 Newton is applied over a distance of 1 meter. One joule (J) equals one kilogram-meter squared per second squared ($kg \cdot m^2/s^2$).

Potential energy is stored energy and kinetic energy is the energy of motion. Together, these two types of energy combine to form the mechanical energy of an object. Mechanical energy can be all kinetic energy, all potential energy, or a combination of both types of energy. Energy can be exerted as a force acting on an object.

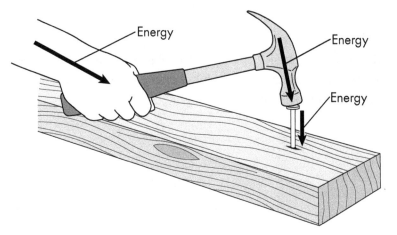

Forces

A force is a push or a pull exerted on an object. For example, you exert a force when you kick a soccer ball or when you pull on a rope. If two objects are touching when a force is exerted, then the force is a contact force. However, if a force is exerted over distance without the objects touching, the force is a field force.

There are four fundamental field forces in nature: gravity, the electromagnetic force, the strong nuclear force, and the weak nuclear force. These forces vary in strength and the distance over which they can affect an object. The strong nuclear force holds protons and neutrons together in the nucleus of an atom. This is the strongest of all forces, but it acts only over distances the size of an atomic nucleus. The weak nuclear force is involved in nuclear reactions, and it acts over even smaller distances than the strong nuclear force. The electromagnetic force is weaker than the strong nuclear force, but it acts over large distances. The gravitational force is much weaker than the electromagnetic force, and it is noticeable over smaller distances than the electromagnetic force.

Isaac Newton developed three laws of motion that helped explain how objects react when various forces are applied. Newton's first law states that an object at rest will stay at rest and an object in motion will stay in motion unless acted upon by an unbalanced force. Newton's second law states that the acceleration of an object is proportional to the force acting on it, or force equals mass times acceleration. Finally, Newton's third law states that all forces act in pairs. In other words, for every action force, there is a reaction force.

If the application of a force results in motion, then the force has performed work. And if work is performed, then energy is expended. Thus, energy and forces are related through the transfer and transformation of one type of energy to another through forces and work.

Physical Science
Core Skills Science, Grade 8

Potential Energy

Potential energy is stored energy. Kinetic energy is the energy of motion. How are these two forms of energy related? All moving objects have kinetic energy. Like all forms of energy, kinetic energy can be used to do work. The faster something is moving, the more kinetic energy it has. Also, the greater the mass of a moving object, the greater its kinetic energy is.

Potential energy is stored energy. It is the energy an object has because of its position. For example, a stretched bow has potential energy because work has been done to change its shape. The energy of that work is turned into potential energy.

When you lift an object, you do work on it. You use a force that is against the force of gravity. When you do this, you transfer energy to the object and give the object gravitational potential energy. Books on a shelf have gravitational potential energy. The amount of gravitational potential energy that an object has depends on its mass and its height.

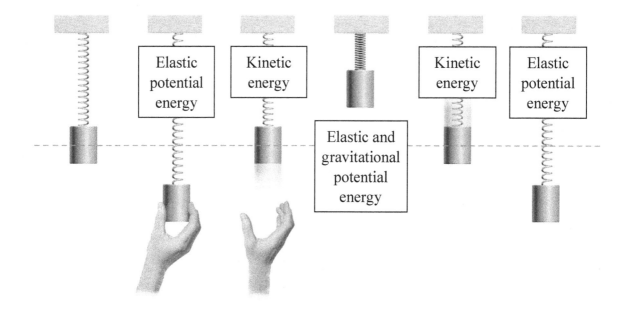

Energy Can Be Transferred and Transformed

Energy can be transferred between two interacting objects by forces. For example, when you apply a force to lift an object off the ground, you are increasing the potential energy of the object.

An energy transformation is a change from one form of energy to another. Any form of energy can change into any other form of energy. For example, kinetic energy can change into potential energy, and vice versa. Chemical energy in food can be converted into energy that your body can use, and chemical energy in fuels can be converted into thermal energy by burning the fuels. Plants convert light energy into chemical energy during photosynthesis.

According to the law of conservation of energy, energy cannot be created or destroyed. The total amount of energy in a closed system is always the same. Energy can change from one form to another, but all of the different forms of energy in a system always add up to the same total amount of energy.

How Are Energy and Forces Related?

Write answers to the questions on the lines below.

1. What is a contact force?

   _____

2. How can energy be transferred?

   _____

   _____

3. What is mechanical energy?

   _____

   _____

4. Who developed laws of motion that help explain the behavior of objects when a force is applied?

   _____

   _____

5. What is a field force?

   _____

6. What is the SI unit of work?

   _____

7. What is energy?

   _____

8. **Main Idea** How are energy and forces related?

   _____

   _____

   _____

   _____

9. **Vocabulary** Describe mechanical energy using the terms *potential energy* and *kinetic energy*.

_____

_____

_____

10. **Reading Skill: Compare and Contrast** What is the difference between energy and forces?

_____

_____

_____

11. **Critical Thinking: Categorize** List the four fundamental forces in order of increasing distance over which they can act.

_____

_____

12. **Inquiry Skill: Apply** Is kicking a ball an example of a contact force or a field force?

_____

13. **Test Prep** Which of the following is NOT an example of potential energy?

   A a drawn bow

   B a ball on a shelf

   C a stretched spring

   D a ball on the ground

What Is a Simple Machine?

Work

Work is defined as the transfer of energy to an object by the application of a force that causes the object to move in the same direction as the applied force. The amount of work done is calculated by multiplying the force by the distance over which the force is applied. The force used to calculate work must be applied in the direction of the object's motion.

$$work = force \times distance$$

Work is calculated as force times distance, with units of newtons times meters (N • m). This combination of SI units is also called joules (J). One joule is equal to one kilogram times one meter squared per second squared ($1\ J = 1\ N \cdot 1\ m = 1\ kg \cdot 1\ m^2/s^2$). You do about 1 J of work when you lift an apple, which weighs about 1 N, from your arm's length down at your side to the top of your head, a distance of about 1 m.

Power

Time does not determine how much work can be done. Running up a flight of stairs quickly does not require more work than walking up slowly does. However, running is more exhausting than walking because the same amount of work is being done in a shorter time when you run. The amount of time that a given amount of work takes is an important factor when you consider work and machines. Power is the rate at which work is done, or how much work is done in a given amount of time.

$$power = work \div time$$

The SI unit of power is the watt (W). One watt is the amount of power needed to do one joule of work in one second. It is about equal to the power needed to lift an apple over your head in 1 s. Power is often expressed in units of 1,000 watts, or 1 kilowatt (kW).

Simple Machine

How do simple machines make work easier? First of all, simple machines include levers, inclined planes, wedges, screws, and wheels and axles. Work is calculated by multiplying the amount of force applied by the distance of motion. Simple machines make work easier by changing the force, distance, or direction of the work. The mechanical advantage of a machine is defined as the output force divided by the input force, or the input distance divided by the output distance. If there is a change in direction but not in distance or force, the mechanical advantage is equal to 1.

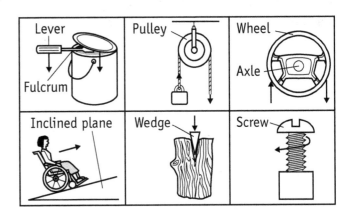

Examples of Simple Machines

When you open window blinds by pulling on a cord, you're using a pulley. A pulley is a simple machine that has a grooved wheel that holds a rope or a cable. A load is attached to one end of the rope, and an input force is applied to the other end. A fixed pulley is attached to something that does not move. By using a fixed pulley, you can pull down on the rope to lift the load up. The pulley changes the direction of the force. Elevators make use of fixed pulleys.

Unlike fixed pulleys, movable pulleys are attached to the object being moved. A movable pulley does not change a force's direction. Movable pulleys do increase force, but they also increase the distance over which the input force must be exerted. When a fixed pulley and a movable pulley are used together, the pulley system is called a block and tackle. The mechanical advantage of a block and tackle depends on the number of rope segments.

An inclined plane is a simple machine that is a straight, slanted surface. A ramp is an inclined plane. Using an inclined plane to load a piano into a truck is easier than lifting the piano into the truck. Rolling the piano along an inclined plane requires a smaller input force than is needed to lift the piano into the truck. The same work is done on the piano, just over a longer distance.

Efficiency

Because of friction and other factors, only some of the work done by a machine is applied to the task at hand. The machine also does some incidental work that does not serve any intended purpose. There is a difference between the total work and the useful work done by a machine.

The efficiency of a machine is a measure of how much useful work a machine can do. Efficiency is defined as the ratio of useful work output to total work input.

$$efficiency = useful\ work\ output \div work\ input$$

Efficiency is usually expressed as a percentage. To change an answer found by using the efficiency equation into a percentage, multiply the answer by 100 and then add the percent sign (%). A machine that is 100% efficient would produce exactly as much useful work as the work done on the machine. Because every machine has some friction, no machine is 100% efficient. The useful work output of a machine never equals or exceeds the work input.

The efficiency of machines can be improved by reducing the friction produced by the machine. Efficiency may also be improved by making a machine more aerodynamic.

What Is a Simple Machine?

Write answers to the questions on the lines below.

1. What would be the mechanical efficiency, as a percentage, of a machine that produced an output of 200 J with an input of 250 J?

   _____

2. How is work calculated?

   _____

   _____

3. A ramp is an example of which type of machine?

   _____

4. What term describes the rate at which work is done?

   _____

5. Describe two ways in which the efficiency of a machine may be improved.

   _____

   _____

6. What is a watt?

   _____

   _____

7. What is mechanical advantage?

   _____

   _____

8. **Main Idea** What is a simple machine?

   _____

   _____

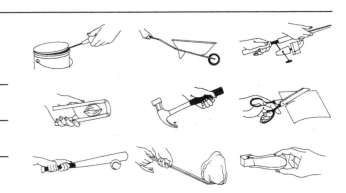

Physical Science
Core Skills Science, Grade 8

9. **Vocabulary** Write a sentence using the terms *energy*, *work*, and *simple machine*.

_____

_____

_____

10. **Reading Skill: Compare and Contrast** What is the difference between work and power?

_____

_____

_____

11. **Critical Thinking: Apply** Sam exerted an average force of 30 N to move a piano. How much work was required to move the piano forward 6 M in 10 s?

_____

_____

_____

12. **Inquiry Skill: Use Numbers** A forklift raises a box above the floor and does 2,000 J of work. If the forklift motor consumes 3,000 J of electrical energy from the battery to raise the box, what is the efficiency of the lift? Show your calculations.

13. **Test Prep** A cyclist does 4.5×10^5 J of work pedaling to the top of a ridge. She completes the climb in 75 s. What is her power output during her ride to the top?

   A 6.0×10^3 kW

   B 6.0 kW

   C 17 kW

   D 3.4×10^4 kW

What Are Seismic Waves?

Mechanical Waves

Waves transfer energy as they travel, and waves can do work. Most waves transfer energy by the vibration of particles in a medium. A medium is a substance through which a wave can travel. A medium can be a solid, a liquid, or a gas. When a particle vibrates, it can pass its energy to a particle next to it. The second particle will vibrate like the first particle. In this way, energy is transmitted through a medium. Waves that need a medium are called mechanical waves. Mechanical waves carry energy from one place to another through the vibration of the particles of the medium.

Seismic waves are a type of mechanical wave. Seismology is the study of earthquakes and the movement of seismic waves through Earth. There are many scientific instruments used to measure seismic waves, including seismographs and seismometers.

Seismic Waves

Seismic waves are mechanical waves that travel through Earth. The speed and direction of seismic waves in Earth depends on the various materials that make up Earth's interior, including the composition of these materials and the state of matter of the layers. Scientists use information about how seismic waves travel through Earth to explain the composition of Earth's interior, even though it cannot be observed directly.

There are two main types of seismic waves. Surface waves move along Earth's surface and body waves move through Earth's interior.

Surface Waves

Surface waves travel along Earth's surface. Surface waves are slower than body waves, but they produce most of the damage associated with seismic waves from earthquakes or volcanic eruptions. There are two types of surface seismic waves: Love waves and Rayleigh waves.

Love waves, named for the British mathematician A. E. H. Love, are the fastest surface wave. Love waves move the ground side to side.

Rayleigh waves, named for the mathematician John William Strutt (Lord Rayleigh), roll through the ground similarly to the way an ocean wave moves through the water. Rayleigh waves move the ground up and down and side to side in the direction of movement of the wave. Shaking during an earthquake is due to Rayleigh waves.

Body Waves

Body waves travel more quickly than surface waves. There are two types of body waves. P waves (primary waves or pressure waves) are body waves that travel more quickly, while S waves (secondary waves or shear waves) are body waves that travel more slowly.

P waves are also known as primary waves, since they travel faster and are the seismic waves that are first detected by sensors. P waves are also known as pressure waves because they result in the alternating compression and extension of material as they travel through a medium. The motion of the medium is forward and backward in relation to the direction of movement of the P wave. P waves can move through both the solid and liquid portions of Earth's interior.

S waves are known as secondary waves, since they travel slower and are recorded after P waves by sensors. S waves are also known as shear waves. S waves result in the side-to-side or up-and-down motion of material in relation to the direction of movement of the S wave. S waves can move only through solid rock, not through liquid rock. Scientists have concluded that Earth's outer core is liquid because of the way S waves are transmitted through Earth's interior.

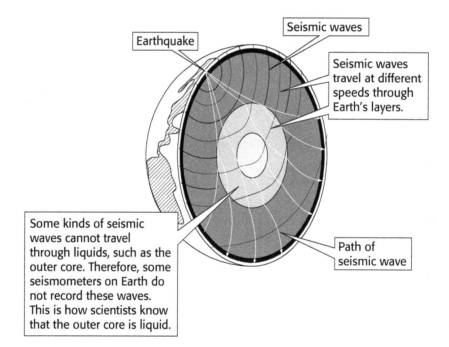

Earthquake

Seismic waves

Seismic waves travel at different speeds through Earth's layers.

Some kinds of seismic waves cannot travel through liquids, such as the outer core. Therefore, some seismometers on Earth do not record these waves. This is how scientists know that the outer core is liquid.

Path of seismic wave

Causes of Seismic Waves

Seismic waves can be produced through natural events such as earthquakes and volcanic eruptions as energy is released in Earth's crust. Humans may also cause seismic waves intentionally or unintentionally. Seismic waves may be an unintended side effect of drilling, mining, or blasting activities. Sometimes, scientists use explosives to intentionally create seismic waves that will be studied to determine the consistency and depths of Earth's layers. Seismic waves are also used to study the characteristics of oil deposits.

What Are Seismic Waves?

Match each term to its correct definition.

Definitions

_____ **1.** mechanical wave that moves along or through Earth

_____ **2.** surface wave that rolls through the ground

_____ **3.** type of seismic wave that travels along Earth's surface

_____ **4.** type of seismic wave that travels through Earth's interior

_____ **5.** slower body waves, also called secondary waves

_____ **6.** fastest surface wave

_____ **7.** faster body waves, also called primary waves

Terms

a. body wave

b. Love wave

c. seismic wave

d. P wave

e. surface wave

f. S wave

g. Rayleigh wave

8. Main Idea What are seismic waves?

_____

_____

_____

_____

_____

_____

_____

_____

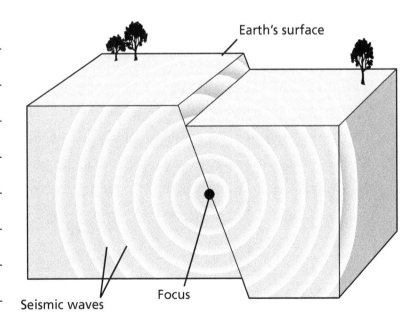

Earth's surface

Seismic waves   Focus

Physical Science
Core Skills Science, Grade 8

9. **Vocabulary** Write a sentence about seismic waves using the terms *P wave*, *S wave*, *Love wave*, and *Rayleigh wave*.

_____

_____

_____

10. **Reading Skill: Main Idea and Details** What do mechanical waves carry?

_____

_____

11. **Critical Thinking: Evaluate** Why is the fact that S waves cannot move through liquid important to scientists who study Earth's interior?

_____

_____

_____

12. **Inquiry Skill: Predict** An earthquake occurs 200 kilometers from the nearest seismograph. Which type of wave will be the first to reach the sensor? Explain your answer.

_____

_____

_____

13. **Test Prep** How does a wave transfer energy through a medium?

    A The particles in the medium vibrate.

    B The wave moves between the particles of the medium.

    C The wave gains energy from the particles in the medium.

    D The particles in the medium move in the direction of the wave.

What Is Digital Technology?

Technology

Logical thinking is not the only skill used in science. Scientists depend on observations and data. Scientists use scientific tools, such as computers, telescopes, and measuring devices with very sensitive sensors. These tools are examples of technology. Technology is the application of science for practical uses.

Engineers look for ways to use science and technology together. Science and technology depend on each other. The first computers filled up a whole room. But advances in science have led to smaller computers that are both faster and cheaper. Modern computers also help scientists. For example, computers help scientists make complex calculations quickly. Because of the development of more powerful computers, scientists are able to process large amounts of data from many different variables. Climate research is an example of a field of science that relies on computers. Mathematical models of Earth's systems do not make exact predictions about future climates, but they do estimate what might happen. Someday, these models may help scientists prevent serious climate problems, such as global warming or another ice age.

In addition to technology and instruments, another important tool of science is mathematics. Most research includes measurements, but measurement data alone do not provide enough information. The data must be analyzed to find relationships between variables. This analysis normally includes mathematical calculations. Much of the value of computers in scientific research is their ability to perform many complicated calculations in a tiny fraction of the time that would be needed without the computers.

Digital Technology

For centuries, digital meant the use of numbers. The term came from digit, or finger, the tool people often used for counting. Today, *digital* is synonymous with *computer*. Any system is said to be using digital technology if it relies on parts that use binary logic. Basic binary logic relies on combinations of the digits 0 and 1, also called bits, that stand for words, numbers, and images. Today, most systems that use digital technology include a microprocessor, some form of storage, and a software program designed for decision making or information processing.

Digital technology allows huge amounts of information to be compressed, or squeezed together. The compressed information is then placed onto small storage devices, allowing the information to be easily preserved and transported. Examples of digital technology have spread into every aspect of modern life. Cellular telephone and cable systems, commercial digital television and radio broadcasts, digital printing, and digital cameras are common examples.

Digital technology has resulted in greater interconnectedness, easier communication, and greater availability of information. These factors allow vast amounts of information to be available to anyone with internet access. The Internet is a global system of connected computer networks. Email, instant messaging, texting, and social media allow friends and even strangers to share information and experiences in a flash. Images of news events, such as protest demonstrations, are instantly available, often out of reach of oppressive governments. Further, digital technology makes both data and research results readily available at very low cost all over the world.

Access to Information

Dissemination, or distribution, has also been greatly changed by digital technology. Current technology is moving toward the virtual product, a product that is completely digitized. A copy of a book, music, or a movie can be sent electronically anywhere, again and again, without needing to restock inventory. What's more, each copy is exactly like every other copy without loss of clarity.

There are, however, some significant negative effects of the increased availability and dissemination of information. Minors with access to digital technology may become vulnerable to internet predators. In some cases, people are not conscious of the extent to which their personal communications may be viewed by the population at large.

The ability of individuals and organizations to publish on any topic to a global audience, at a negligible cost, is also a growing concern. The amount of content relating to illegal and harmful topics such as child pornography, bomb building, calls to terrorism, and other violent activities led some people to lobby for censorship and regulation. Plagiarism, copyright infringement, and outright theft of intellectual property is on the rise. The widespread ability of consumers to produce and distribute exact reproductions of protected works has become a major legal issue, particularly for musicians and filmmakers.

Technology and Privacy

Finally, privacy has become a concern with users of digital technology. Banks, credit agencies, marketing firms, and even game sites store a tremendous amount of personal information. Consumers continually ask what these entities do with all that private information, and they worry that the information may be packaged and marketed. In addition, hackers are becoming more and more sophisticated, increasing the incidence of identity theft. As dependence on and use of digital technology grows, the advantages and disadvantages grow as well.

What Is Digital Technology?

Write answers to the questions on the lines below.

1. Name three digital technologies that offer greater personal interconnectedness.

   _____

2. What is technology?

   _____

   _____

3. What are the three components of a digital system?

   _____

   _____

4. What is a virtual product?

   _____

5. What are the benefits of compressing information for storage?

   _____

6. What is the Internet?

   _____

7. **Main Idea** What is digital technology?

   _____

   _____

   _____

   _____

   _____

   _____

Physical Science
Core Skills Science, Grade 8

8. Vocabulary Write a sentence using the terms *digital* and *bit*.

_____

_____

9. Reading Skill: Main Idea and Details How does climate research depend on digital technology?

_____

_____

_____

10. Critical Thinking: Synthesis Using computers as an example, explain how science and technology depend on each other.

_____

_____

_____

11. Inquiry Skill: Compare List three advantages and three disadvantages of digital technology. Do you think the advantages of digital technology outweigh the disadvantages? Provide support for your answer.

_____

_____

_____

_____

12. Test Prep Which of these would not be an example of technology?

    A electron microscope

    B earthquake waves

    C computer

    D microwave towers

How Are Models Used by Scientists and Engineers?

Models

A model is a representation of an object or a system. A model uses something familiar to help you understand something that is not familiar. For example, models of human organs can demonstrate how the body works. Models can also be used to explain the past and the present, such as a computer model of how the universe formed. They can even be used to predict future events.

Models are used in science to help explain how something works or to describe how something is structured. Models are used in engineering to test and evaluate different solutions.

Models can also be used to make predictions or to explain observations. However, models have limitations. A model is never exactly like the real thing—if it were, it would no longer be a model. There are many types of models, including physical models, mathematical models, and conceptual models. Physical models include replicas that can be seen or touched. Mathematical models include sets of equations or computer simulations that generate data that mimic real-world events. Conceptual models can be analogies—verbal or visual comparisons of things that are known and things that are unknown. Models can also combine different model types.

Physical Models

Physical models are typically a larger or smaller version of an actual object. A model rocket and a plastic atomic model are examples of physical models. The model rocket is smaller than the real rocket, and the atomic model is larger than the real atom. Many physical models look like the thing they model. However, a limitation of the model of a body is that it is not alive and doesn't act exactly like a human body. But the model is useful for understanding how the body works. Other physical models may look and act more like or less like the thing they represent than the model does. Scientists often use the model that is simplest to use but that still serves their purpose.

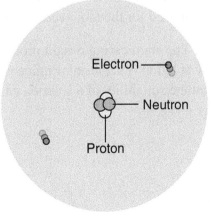

Mathematical Models

A mathematical model may be made up of numbers, equations, or other forms of data. Some mathematical models are simple and can be used easily. A Punnett square is a model of how traits may be passed from parents to offspring. Using this model, scientists can predict how often certain traits will appear in the offspring of certain parents. Computers are very useful for creating and manipulating mathematical models. They make fewer mistakes and can keep track of more variables than a human can. But a computer model can be incorrect in many ways. The more complex a model is, the more carefully scientists must build the model.

Conceptual Models

A third type of model is the conceptual model. Conceptual models are different from physical models in that they exist only in the mind, or as a description. There is not a solid object that represents the model. This is necessary because sometimes conceptual models represent systems of ideas that cannot be modeled by a physical model. Others compare unfamiliar things with familiar things. These comparisons help explain unfamiliar ideas. The idea that life originated from chemicals is a conceptual model. Scientists also use conceptual models to classify behaviors of animals. Scientists can then predict how an animal might respond to a certain action based on the behaviors that have already been observed.

Models in Engineering

An important part of the engineering design process is testing and evaluating solutions to determine which best solve the problem while meeting all constraints. Engineers build models of proposed solutions in order to test and evaluate the solution.

Engineers may use different kinds of models. Mathematical models on a computer may be used to model the parameters and constraints of a new bridge construction project. This model may help an engineer approve a bridge design or decide on a certain material for the bridge. Engineers often build physical models if model size does not preclude this option. Physical models may be built to test a tool or part of a machine to make sure it functions properly and has the needed lifespan. For example, an engineer may test whether a new bottle opener can efficiently open 100 bottles. If the opener breaks after only 50 bottles, then either the tool design or the material used for the tool needs to be reevaluated.

It is important that models be accurate. The engineering design process is an iterative process, which means it is repeated until a satisfactory solution is achieved. Engineers depend on quality data to make sound decisions. A good decision about the suitability of a solution cannot be made if the model used to depict the solution is inaccurate.

How Are Models Used by Scientists and Engineers?

Write answers to the questions on the lines below.

1. Name two examples of a physical model.

_____

2. What does it mean that engineering is an iterative process?

_____

_____

3. How are models used in science?

_____

_____

4. What is a mathematical model?

_____

_____

5. Why is it important that engineering models be accurate?

_____

_____

6. Are all physical models the same size as the object they are modeling?

_____

_____

7. What is a model?

_____

8. **Main Idea** How do engineers use models?

_____

_____

_____

127

9. Vocabulary Describe a relationship between engineering and science using the term *model*.

_____

_____

10. Reading Skill: Main Idea and Details Describe three types of scientific models.

_____

_____

_____

11. Critical Thinking: Synthesize Why do scientists and engineers use models in different ways?

_____

_____

_____

_____

12. Inquiry Skill: Predict Which type of model would a scientist studying hurricanes most likely use to predict the occurrence of future storms?

_____

_____

_____

13. Test Prep What is a limitation of models?

    A A model is never exactly like the real thing.

    B Models cannot be built using computers.

    C You cannot hold any type of model.

    D Models cannot be used to explain systems of ideas.

Answer Key

How Do Animals Reproduce?
LS1.B

1. Two parents are need to produce a baby tiger through sexual reproduction.
2. Animals lack a cell wall and are heterotrophs, meaning they cannot produce their own food.
3. Human body cells have 23 pairs of chromosomes.
4. Sexual reproduction results in increased genetic diversity.
5. Asexual reproduction allows organisms to reproduce without finding a mate.
6. Budding occurs when smaller, genetically identical offspring split, or bud, from the parent organism.
7. The majority of animals reproduce through sexual reproduction.
8. Animals can reproduce by sexual or asexual reproduction.
9. Cell division by meiosis results in haploid sex cells, which are necessary for sexual reproduction.
10. Each human sex cell contains 23 chromosomes. The cell formed when the sex cells unite will have 46 total chromosomes, or 23 pairs of chromosomes.
11. Sexual reproduction involves the joining of two parent cells to produce offspring. Sexual reproduction works because the sex cells that are joined were produced through meiosis, which means they have half the number of chromosomes. If organisms reproduced through sexual reproduction without producing sex cells through meiosis, then the chromosome number of the offspring would be double that of the parent organisms.
12. Student diagrams should accurately show the number of chromosomes for parent and offspring organisms, and sex cells where appropriate.
13. D

What Is Cellular Respiration?
LS1.C; PS3.D

1. cellular respiration
2. reactants
3. carbon dioxide, water, energy
4. Metabolism
5. ATP
6. anaerobic
7. energy, matter
8. Cellular respiration is the process cells use to harvest the energy in organic compounds, particularly glucose. Cellular respiration uses sugar and oxygen gas as the reactants to produce energy, water, and carbon dioxide.
9. Animals cannot make their own food like plants can, so animals get nutrition and energy by eating plants or other animals. Plants produce food by capturing the energy in sunlight during photosynthesis. When an animal eats a plant or another animal that has eaten a plant, the stored sugar molecules are broken down during a series of steps known as cellular respiration. Cellular respiration stores the energy from food in ATP molecules that are used as "energy currency" within cells.
10. ATP, or adenosine triphosphate, is made up of an adenine, a ribose sugar, and three phosphate groups.
11. Bacteria do not have mitochondria, and so cellular respiration in bacteria cannot occur within the mitochondria. Therefore, the chemical reactions for cellular respiration in bacteria occur within the cell membranes.
12. Students should draw a diagram that indicates that cellular respiration and photosynthesis have a cyclic relationship. The products of one process are used as the reactants in the other.
13. C

How Are Populations Modeled?
LS2.A

1. g
2. d
3. f
4. b
5. h
6. a
7. e
8. c
9. When scientists predict how a population will change, they make a model of the population. The model attempts to exhibit the key characteristics of a real population. By making a change in the model and observing the outcome, scientists can predict what might occur in a real population.
10. A simple population growth model describes the rate of population growth as the difference between the birthrate and the death rate. Exponential population growth model is characterized by a constant rate of population growth which results in a steady, exponential increase in population size. The logistic model is a population model in which exponential growth is limited by a density-dependent factor.
11. organism, population, community, ecosystem, biosphere
12. The population growth rate is the birthrate minus the death rate (r = birthrate – death rate).
13. Resources in the ecosystem will become more abundant with the removal of the third species. In particular, it will be easier for species one to find the fruit it prefers, and it will be easier for species two to find the seeds it prefers.
14. C

How Do Ecosystems Change?
LS2.C
1. pioneer
2. primary
3. Succession
4. ecosystem
5. faster
6. Secondary
7. climax
8. The process of succession is usually triggered by a disturbance in an ecosystem, whether it be a volcanic eruption that triggers primary succession or a flood that triggers secondary succession.
9. Succession is the gradual change of a community over time. Primary succession begins with pioneer species and culminates in a stable community known as a climax community.
10. Secondary succession can be triggered by a disturbance to an ecosystem, such as a flood, an earthquake, or the abandonment of farmland by humans.
11. Pioneer species physically and chemically break down rocks and help begin the process of soil formation. As pioneer species die and decay, the nutrients in their remains enrich the newly forming soil.
12. The new island would undergo primary succession, so the island should show signs of pioneer species, such as lichens.
13. B

How Do Animals Interact in Groups? LS2.D (HIGH SCHOOL)
1. The two types of behavior are innate behavior and learned behavior.
2. An innate defensive behavior in rabbits is the instinct to freeze in the presence of a predator.
3. Some monkeys learn to forage more successfully by using sticks as tools to increase access to insects.
4. Disadvantages to living in groups include increased spread of disease and the possibility of decreased reproductive opportunities.
5. Advantages to living in groups include increased foraging or hunting success and decreased predation risk.
6. Chickens use a pecking order to rank group members from most dominant to most subordinate.
7. A social group is a collection of individuals.
8. Animals interact in groups through social behavior, such as dominance and reconciliatory behaviors, cooperative behaviors, marking territories, mating, and playing.
9. An instinct is an innate behavior that is part of an animal's inherited traits, while a learned behavior must be learned through experience or watching other individuals.
10. An example of cooperative behavior in animals is hunting together to increase hunting success, or foraging together using a system of lookouts and alarm calls to increase foraging efficiency.
11. An example of a human group based on genetic relatedness is an immediate family in which parents live together with children. An example of a human group based on proximity could be a group of college students living in a dorm. They may not be related to one another, but they live together in a group based on where they go to school.
12. There are disadvantages to forming groups, such as the possibility of decreased reproductive opportunities. However, since animals have evolved to be best suited to their environments, it is logical to reason that animals forming

groups is the most beneficial arrangement possible. In other words, the evolutionary advantages must outweigh the evolutionary disadvantages.
13. D

How Are Traits Inherited?
LS3.A
1. g
2. a
3. f
4. e
5. c
6. d
7. b
8. When organisms reproduce, they pass copies of their DNA on to their offspring. This passing of genetic materials is called heredity.
9. An organism's genotype is the set of alleles that an individual has for a characteristic. An organism's phenotype is the expression of the set of alleles for a characteristic. Genotype is the genetic information, and phenotype is the trait that results from the genetic information.
10. In simple inheritance, a dominant allele is always expressed over a recessive allele. This means that the trait of a recessive allele will be expressed only if an organism has two copies of the recessive allele and no copies of the dominant allele.
11. Genes are specific segments of DNA at specific locations on specific chromosomes. The expressed traits of an organism result from protein production based on the specific nucleotide sequence of genes.
12. The nucleotide sequence of a gene is very important because it provides the information for the synthesis of specific proteins, which in turn affects the traits expressed by an organism. If the nucleotide

sequence changes, the correct protein may not be produced.

13. D

What Are Genetic Mutations?
LS3.B

1. Mutations in sex cells can produce new alleles in natural populations.
2. An inversion mutation occurs when a segment of DNA reattaches to the original chromosome but in a reverse orientation.
3. Genes provide information for the production of specific proteins.
4. A point mutation is the change of one nucleotide in a segment of DNA.
5. Mutations are relatively rare.
6. Exposure to radiation and some chemicals can cause mutations.
7. Mutations must occur in sex cells to be passed to future generations. Mutations in body cells only affect the individual organism.
8. Genetic mutations are changes to the DNA sequence of a gene.
9. A gene alteration occurs when a mutation changes the protein output of a gene. Alterations are beneficial if they result in a change that increases an organism's chance of survival and reproduction. Alterations are harmful if they result in a change that decreases an organism's chance of survival and reproduction, or outright kill the organism. Alterations are neutral if they have no effect on the survival and reproductive success of an organism.
10. Genetic mutations provide genetic diversity because mutation is one way that new variations, or alleles, are formed. For organisms that live in changing environments, it is important to have a high level of diversity because it gives a species a better chance of being able to adapt to changing conditions that may otherwise decimate a genetically identical population.
11. A mutation may be neutral if it occurs in a region of DNA that does not code for a gene. It may also be neutral if the organism has a copy of the correct gene that can cover for the mutated gene.
12. A deletion mutation has occurred because the Mutant sequence is missing a G. There should be a G at the ninth character from the left of the sequence.
13. D

What Is the Fossil Record?
LS4.A

1. radioactive decay
2. geologic column
3. Extinction
4. incomplete
5. sediment
6. absolute
7. Relative
8. The fossil record contains all of the fossils that exist on Earth. The fossil record represents a record of living things from Earth's history.
9. Absolute dating provides a way for scientists to assign a numeric age to a fossil, while relative dating is used to assign an age to a fossil that is relative to other objects in the fossil record.
10. Conditions in which an organism is quickly buried by fine sediments may cause a fossil to form. These conditions may occur in wet lowlands, slow-moving streams, lakes, shallow streams, or near volcanoes.
11. A scientist would be unable to date a fossil using radiometric dating if there were no radioactive isotopes in the rock in which the fossil formed.
12. Students should draw a geologic column with five layers. The layers should be numbered from bottom to top, starting with 1 and ending with 5.
13. A

What Is Natural Selection?
LS4.B

1. Overproduction is the production of more offspring than the environment can support.
2. Darwin first proposed the theory of evolution through natural selection.
3. An adaptation is an inherited trait that has become common in a population because the trait provides a selective advantage.
4. Genetic variation is necessary for natural selection to occur because there must be some differences in the population to be selected for or against.
5. Natural selection will suppress an unfavorable trait.
6. Environmental factors determine which traits in a population are favorable.
7. Individuals do not evolve. The evolution of a species takes place at the population level as favorable traits become more common over many generations.
8. Natural selection is the increased reproductive success that arises because an individual is better adapted to its environment than other individuals in the population.
9. Evolution is a change in the genetic characteristics of a population from one generation to the next. Evolution occurs through the process of natural selection, or the increased reproductive success of well-adapted individuals.
10. The four components of natural selection are overproduction, genetic variation, competition, and reproductive success.

11. These behaviors increase within a population because the well-adapted individuals with the behaviors reproduce more frequently than others in the population.

12. Bird A has a bill adapted for eating only seeds. The disappearance of insects would least affect Bird A.

13. B

How Do New Species Form?
LS4.C

1. Speciation
2. Natural selection
3. subspecies
4. gradualism
5. divergence
6. punctuated equilibrium
7. Over time, populations of the same species that differ genetically because of adaptations to different living conditions become what biologists call subspecies. Eventually, the subspecies may become so different that they can no longer interbreed successfully. Biologists then consider them separate species.
8. Punctuated equilibrium is the theory that evolution occurs in spurts separated by periods of little or no change. Major environmental changes in the past are the primary cause of punctuated equilibrium.
9. The fossil record provides evidence of punctuated equilibrium.
10. Another example of adaptive radiation in the animal kingdom is that of birds. Many different species of bird have developed from a common ancestral species to fill many niches throughout Earth's ecosystems.
11. Divergence is the accumulation of genetic differences between two groups. Eventually, if there is enough divergence, the groups will form two different species, which is the process of speciation.

12. C

How Are Stars Classified?
ESS1.A

1. The star is likely composed primarily of hydrogen and helium.
2. A light year is the distance that light travels through empty space in a year.
3. A spectrograph breaks a star's light into a spectrum.
4. A Hertzsprung-Russell diagram compares the temperature and luminosity of stars.
5. A constellation is a pattern in the stars.
6. A hot star with a low luminosity would be a white dwarf on the Hertzsprung-Russell diagram.
7. Emission lines are made when certain wavelengths of light, or colors, are given off by hot gases.
8. Stars appear to move due to the rotation of Earth on its axis and the revolution of Earth in its orbit around the sun.
9. Scientists can decide whether a star is on or off the main sequence depicted by the Hertzsprung-Russell diagram by estimating the star's temperature and luminosity. Scientists can determine the composition and temperature of a star by observing its absorption spectrum. And scientists can describe how far away a star is using the unit of light years.
10. When almost all the hydrogen is used up in a star about the size of the sun, its core contracts. Hydrogen fusion continues in the outer shell as it expands and cools. These stars begin to glow with a reddish color and are known as giants.
11. The sun's two major spectral lines are from hydrogen and helium, since these elements make up 99% of the mass of the

sun. The sun also shows other spectral lines because it has traces of all other elements.

12. The upper-right section of the Hertzsprung-Russell diagram is an area for stars with cooler temperatures and high luminosity. A star could move toward this area when hydrogen is almost depleted. Hydrogen fusion continues in the outer shell as it expands and cools. Some stars, like Betelgeuse, grow to 1,000 times greater than the size of the sun. However, because their surface areas have expanded, their surface temperatures are relatively cool.

13. C

What Is the Earth-Moon System? ESS1.A

1. 28
2. gravity
3. Regolith
4. Synchronous
5. tides
6. Neil Armstrong
7. 3500
8. The Earth-Moon system consists of Earth, the moon, and all of the interactions between the two bodies.
9. Observers on Earth always see the same face of the moon due to the moon's synchronous orbit. The appearance of the moon changes over a 28-day cycle due to the phases of the moon. The phases of the moon are a result of the changes in the relative positions of Earth and the sun.
10. During a waxing moon, the sunlit part of the moon is increasing. During a waning moon, the sunlit part of the moon is decreasing.
11. The moon stabilizes Earth on its axis, which moderates the climate on Earth. And the moon is the main body responsible for the very regular tides that occur on Earth.

12. 15.5 cm

13. B

How Does Gravity Cause Tides? ESS1.B

1. Milky Way

2. spring

3. tidal barrage

4. tide

5. two

6. high

7. Low

8. The Earth-moon-sun system is formed through gravitational interactions of Earth, the moon, and the sun.

9. Tidal energy is a renewable energy resource that is produced by a tidal barrage across an inlet, or by an underwater turbine.

10. Interactions in the Earth-moon-sun system result in day and night time on Earth, the seasons on Earth, the phases of the moon, and the tides, all of which can be predicted and forecasted with some regularity.

11. Tides are a renewable energy resource because the ocean water used to generate the power is not used up in the process and the tidal motion is an unchanging characteristic of the Earth-moon-sun system.

12. A neap tide occurs when the sun and moon are at right angles to each other in relation to Earth. This means the angle between the sun, moon, and Earth is 90°.

13. A

How Do Seasons Affect Plants and Animals? ESS1.B

1. f

2. g

3. d

4. b

5. c

6. e

7. a

8. Seasons affect plants and animals by eliciting responses or behaviors. For example,

plants respond to changes in the length of day that accompany changes in season. Plants use these cues to reproduce at the best time or to know when to enter dormancy. Animals may migrate, hibernate, or estivate in response to seasonal changes.

9. Estivation and hibernation both involve animals entering a state of torpor, but estivation occurs during the summer season and hibernation occurs during the winter season.

10. Short-day plants flower in fall or winter when the night length is long and the day length is short. Other plants flower in spring or early summer, when night length is short and the day length is long. These plants are called long-day plants.

11. Locations near the equator have approximately the same temperatures and same amount of daylight year round. This means they do not experience all fours seasons in the way that locations in more southern or northern latitudes do.

12. Dormancy in plants is similar to hibernation in animals. Both responses occur during the winter season, and both involve organisms decreasing metabolic activity and conserving energy and resources.

13. D

How Are Materials Dated? ESS1.C

1. Sedimentary

2. carbon-14

3. neutrons

4. absolute

5. isotopes

6. parent, daughter

7. Radiometric dating

8. The law of superposition states that an undisturbed sedimentary rock layer is older than the layers above it and younger than the layers below it. Relative dating uses this

concept to assign relative ages to rock layers and objects found within rock layers, such as fossils.

9. The method of using the steady radioactive decay of isotopes to measure absolute age is called radiometric dating.

10. First, the fossil must be present in rocks scattered over a large region. Second, it must have features that distinguish it from other fossils. Third, the organisms from which the fossil formed must have lived during a short span of geologic time. Fourth, the fossil must occur in fairly large numbers within the rock layer.

11. For radiometric dating to be accurate, the half-life of a measured isotope must be proportional to the time period that the material is being dated to. Isotopes with a longer half-life are used to date older materials.

12. Scientists likely used Uranium-238 to date Earth's age. It decays to lead-206 and has a half-life of 4.5 billion years.

13. B

What Is Evidence of Tectonic Plate Movement? ESS1.C; ESS2.B

1. continental drift

2. Convection

3. mid-ocean ridges

4. ocean trenches

5. faults

6. 5

7. Volcanism

8. The theory of plate tectonics states that Earth's lithosphere is divided into huge slabs of rocks called tectonic plates. The plates move on top of the slowly moving asthenosphere.

9. The movement of tectonic plates causes the formation of mountains through the process of mountain building; volcanism around plate boundaries and hotspots; and earthquakes along plate boundaries.

10. The solid rock of the asthenosphere flows very slowly because of density differences caused by the outward flow of heat from deep within Earth. When rock is heated, it expands, becomes less dense, and tends to rise to the surface of Earth. As the rock gets near the surface, it cools, becomes denser, and tends to sink. This process is called a convection current. Convection currents cause the slow movement of tectonic plates in the lithosphere.

11. One line of evidence that supports the theory of plate tectonics is the fact that corresponding coastlines match up visually and chemically through radiometric dating of rock. A second line of evidence is the presence of similar fossils on continents that are on different sides of the Atlantic Ocean. A third line of evidence is the dating of oceanic lithosphere and the obvious pattern of older rock occurring farther from mid-ocean ridges, and younger rock occurring at mid-ocean ridges.

12. There are 100 cm in 1 m. If a tectonic plate moves 3 cm per year, then it will take the plate 100 years to move 3 m.

13. C

What Are Ocean Currents?
ESS2.C

1. Salinity is a measure of the amount of dissolved salts in water.

2. Earth is referred to as an ocean planet because over 70% of Earth's surface is covered by water.

3. Upwelling often occurs along coastlines where wind pushes surface water that is then replaced by deeper water.

4. The largest oceans on Earth are

the Pacific Ocean, the Atlantic Ocean, the Indian Ocean, and the Arctic Ocean.

5. Other than water, ocean currents transport energy, nutrients, and debris.

6. Successful fisheries may occur near upwellings because the water that rises to the surface is nutrient-rich.

7. Ocean water is saltwater.

8. Ocean currents are stream-like movements of water that transport water and energy around the planet.

9. Thermohaline currents are deep ocean currents that are triggered by differences in water density due to salinity and temperature.

10. Surface and deep ocean currents are alike because they both move ocean water, and therefore thermal energy, around the planet. They are different because surface currents are driven by the wind, while deep currents are driven by water density differences.

11. Density is mass per volume of a substance. Salinity is the amount of dissolved salt in water. Water with a higher salinity has more salt dissolved in it. The dissolved salt adds mass to the water, which increases its density.

12. Global climate change may change global winds, which would affect surface currents. Global climate change may also affect deep ocean currents by changing the temperature of surface water, thereby changing where surface water sinks and deeper water rises.

13. A

What Affects Earth's Climate?
ESS2.D

1. equator
2. Precipitation
3. decreases
4. biome
5. Climatology
6. Wind

7. abiotic

8. Climate refers to the average weather conditions of an area over a period of time.

9. Conditions in the atmosphere, such as precipitation and wind, are typically used to describe weather and climate. Energy in the atmosphere moves through convection currents.

10. Climate is important to humans because it controls access to food, water, and energy. Natural disasters due to climate conditions are also capable of producing widespread damage.

11. Climate is an abiotic factor that determines where species can survive. A biome is an area in which the climate typically determines the plant community, which in turn supports the animal community.

12. Winds are caused by differences in air pressure, which are in turn caused by uneven heating of Earth's surface. If Earth's surface was the same temperature everywhere, there would be no differences in air pressure, and therefore, there would be no wind.

13. A

What Is the Relationship Between Earth and Living Things? ESS2.E (HIGH SCHOOL)

1. carbon dioxide, oxygen
2. Ozone
3. hydrogen, helium
4. bubble model
5. atmosphere
6. hydrosphere
7. primordial soup
8. Earth is a complex system that interacts with living things. The systems on Earth affect living things, such as the destruction of habitat through natural disasters. Living things on Earth can also affect Earth systems, such as the construction of the atmosphere by photosynthetic organisms or the acceleration of climate

change by humans.

9. Earth is a complex system that is made of smaller interacting parts. The geosphere is the solid Earth. The atmosphere is the envelope of gases that surround Earth. The hydrosphere is all of the water on Earth, including water in the atmosphere and water in the oceans. The biosphere is the part of Earth that contains living things.

10. According to the theory, the bubbles in the ancient oceans contained ammonia, methane, and other gases and provided protection from UV radiation. The inorganic molecules reacted and formed complex organic molecules that were then released to the atmosphere.

11. The two models of the origination of life both suggest that complex organic molecules arose from the reaction of inorganic molecules on ancient Earth.

12. Photosynthesizing organisms released oxygen during photosynthesis. The oxygen eventually built up in Earth's atmosphere, creating the mixture and concentration of gases present today.

13. B

What Are Natural Resources?
ESS3.A

1. b
2. f
3. e
4. a
5. d
6. c
7. g
8. A natural resource is any natural material that is used by humans. Examples of natural resources are water, petroleum, minerals, forests, soil, and animals.
9. Solar power and hydropower are both examples of renewable energy resources.
10. A renewable resource is a natural

resource that can be replaced at the same rate at which it is used. A nonrenewable resource is a resource that forms at a rate that is much slower than the rate at which it is consumed.

11. To help conserve water resources, I could remember to turn off the water while I am brushing my teeth. To help conserve energy, I could remember to turn off the light when I leave a room. To help conserve mineral resources, I could recycle aluminum cans and glass.

12. As the global population increases, the global forests may become depleted as more land is cleared for agricultural use. The global freshwater supply may become depleted as more water is needed for human use and agricultural purposes. And oil reserves may become depleted as energy demands increase.

13. A

What Is Sustainability? ESS3.C

1. Fossil fuels are a nonrenewable resource.
2. On average, individuals in developed countries use more resources than individuals in undeveloped countries.
3. Solar energy is renewable.
4. Living roofs provide habitats for living things.
5. Desalination is removing the salt from salt water.
6. Rotational grazing involves moving livestock from one area to another to prevent overgrazing.
7. Fossil fuels can be used to make plastic.
8. Sustainability is the condition in which human society can go on indefinitely and future generations can have a standard of living as high as the present one.
9. Nonrenewable resources are used up more quickly than they

can be replaced, and renewable resources can be replaced as they are used. Sustainability requires the use of renewable resources.

10. Cover crops keep the soil from compacting and washing away, they help the soil absorb water, and they provide habitat for beneficial insects.

11. Possible answer: Energy costs could be significantly less in a green home.

12. Possible answer: Planting cover crops would require extra work.

13. D

How Does Earth's Climate Change? ESS3.D

1. The last ice age reached its peak about 18,000 years ago.
2. Currently, the ice sheets are melting and sea level has been rising at a rate of about 1 mm per year.
3. Climate describes the average weather conditions of an area over a given period of time.
4. Changes in the wobble of Earth's axis can reverse seasons.
5. A glacier is a large body of ice.
6. A period of cooler climate that is characterized by the advancement of glaciers is called a glacial period.
7. Earth is currently in an interglacial period.
8. Natural changes in the shape of Earth's orbit, the tilt of its axis, and the wobble of Earth on its axis occur in regular intervals called Milankovitch cycles, which occur every 21,000 to 100,000 years.
9. An ice age represents a cooler time period on Earth, and it is characterized by glaciation, or the presence of large glaciers on Earth's surface. An interglacial period represents a warmer time period on Earth, and it is characterized by the retreat of glaciers on Earth's surface.
10. Decreasing the tilt of Earth's axis decreases temperature

differences between seasons. The tilt of Earth's axis varies between 22.2° and 24.5°. The greater the tilt of the angle, the more solar energy the poles receive.

11. Milankovitch cycles occur over tens of thousands of years. This time frame is important to the discussion of global climate change because although it is important to know all of the natural factors that can affect the global climate, the current warming trends are occurring too quickly to be attributed to the long-term natural factors, such as the Milankovitch cycle.

12. Rising sea levels are a concern because if they continue to rise, low-lying coastal regions will eventually be underwater. The locations of many large cities, such as New York, Los Angeles, Miami, and Houston, would be submerged.

13. B

What Are States of Matter?
PS1.A
1. g
2. b
3. d
4. e
5. a
6. h
7. c
8. f
9. Matter is anything that has mass and takes up space. The three most common states of matter are solid, liquid, and gas. States of matter are classified based on the energy of the particles and the motion of the particles.

10. States of matter can be defined by describing the motion of particles in each state. In a solid, particles are tightly packed and do not move, though they do vibrate in place. In a liquid, the particles are less tightly packed and are free to move past each other. In a gas, the particles are far apart from one another and

touch only when they collide during their random movements.

11. For a substance to change from a liquid to a gas, energy must be added to a system. For the substance to change back into a liquid from a gas, energy would have to be removed from the system.

12. Bonds between atoms or molecules in a solid are stronger than the bonds in a liquid or gas. This is because the atoms or molecules in a solid are closer together than in a liquid or a gas.

13. If energy is removed from liquid water, it will become a solid, ice. If energy is added to liquid water, it will become a gas, water vapor. These changes represent freezing and vaporization.

14. C

How Are Reference Points Used to Measure Motion? PS2.A
1. Acceleration
2. slope
3. Motion
4. speed
5. m/s
6. straight
7. m/s^2
8. When an object changes position over time, the object is in motion. A stationary reference point is used to gauge direction and speed of motion.

9. Acceleration is the rate at which velocity, or speed in a specific direction, changes.

10. An object's speed is the rate at which its distance is changing compared to a reference point.

11. Acceleration is the rate at which velocity changes, and velocity is a measure of displacement. A stationary object is undergoing no displacement, so its velocity is zero and its acceleration is zero, as well.

12. If the two objects are moving in different directions, they can be traveling at the same speed, but

the velocities will be different since the directions are different.

13. A

What Is Gravity? PS2.B
1. Gravity is the force that keeps galaxies together.

2. The newton, named for Isaac Newton, is the SI unit for weight.

3. The Law of Universal Gravitation is a scientific law because it is a description of observations that are always true. It is not a theory because it does not explain why the attraction between objects is related to mass and distance.

4. An object with the same mass will weigh more on Jupiter than it does on Earth.

5. Mass is a measure of the amount of matter in an object.

6. Inertia is an object's resistance to a change in speed or direction until an outside force acts on the object.

7. The gravitational pull of the sun keeps the planets in orbit around the sun.

8. Objects in the universe attract each other through a gravitational force that depends on their masses and distance between the objects.

9. Mass is the amount of matter in an object. Weight is a measurement of the force of gravity acting on an object. An object's mass is a constant characteristic, but an object's weight can change based on the object's location in the universe.

10. The force of gravity between two objects depends on the mass of the two objects and the distance between the two objects. The gravitation force increases as the masses increase and as the distance between the objects decreases.

11. The mass of the pencil is too small to cause a gravitational attraction large enough for a human to notice.

136

12. $75 \times 1.6 = 120$ N

13. C

What Is Thermal Energy?
PS3.A

1. kinetic
2. thermometer
3. Fahrenheit
4. Pressure
5. specific heat
6. kelvin
7. higher
8. Thermal energy is the energy of motion of the particles of a substance.
9. Thermal energy is all of the kinetic energy caused by the random motion of the particles that make up an object. Temperature is a measure of thermal energy. Temperature is measured with a thermometer.
10. Particles in a gas have more energy than particles in a liquid, which have more energy than particles in a solid.
11. Different temperature scales have been developed throughout history. The Kelvin scale was developed as an absolute scale in which absolute zero is set to zero. The Fahrenheit scale is still commonly used in the United States.
12. There are 100 degrees on the Celsius scale between the freezing point of water and the boiling point of water. Similarly, the difference between the freezing point of water and the boiling point of water on the Kelvin scale is 100. So, one degree Celsius is equal to one interval on the Kelvin scale.
13. B

How Is Energy Transferred?
PS3.B

1. radiation
2. conduction
3. Heat
4. currents
5. higher, lower
6. Convection
7. Image A shows convection.
8. Convection is the transfer of energy through the movement of a liquid or a gas. Conduction is the transfer of energy from one substance to another through direct contact. Radiation is the transfer of energy through electromagnetic waves. One of the biggest differences between the three processes is that radiation can transfer energy through a vacuum, such as when energy from the sun is transferred to Earth.
9. Energy is transferred from the sun to Earth through the process of radiation. Some of this thermal energy is re-reflected and heats the atmosphere by the processes of conduction and convection. Conduction occurs when Earth's surface transfers heat to that part of the atmosphere directly above it. Convection occurs when energy is transferred by the flow of gases in the atmosphere.
10. Convection currents occur within the atmosphere and within Earth as hot materials rise and cold materials sink.
11. The rising of hot material and the falling of cool material describes convection, and more specifically, convection currents.
12. If no transfer of energy is occurring between the spatula and the water, then they must be the same temperature. This means the spatula must be at a temperature of 80°C.
13. C

How Are Energy and Forces Related? PS3.C

1. If two objects are touching when a force is exerted, then the force is a contact force.
2. Energy can be transferred between two interacting objects by forces.
3. Mechanical energy is all the kinetic and potential energy of an object.
4. Isaac Newton developed three laws of motion to help explain how objects react to applied forces.
5. If a force is exerted over a distance without the objects touching, the force is a field force.
6. The SI unit for work is the joule.
7. Energy can be broadly defined as the ability to do work.
8. Energy and forces are related because forces can transfer energy between objects or transform energy from one type to another.
9. The mechanical energy of an object is the sum of the potential energy, or stored energy, and kinetic energy, or energy of motion.
10. Energy is the ability to do work, or to displace an object. A force is a push or pull on an object that may result in the displacement of an object. So, energy is exerted as a force to do work on an object.
11. In order of increasing distance over which they can act, the four fundamental forces are the weak nuclear force, the strong nuclear force, the gravitational force, and the electromagnetic force.
12. Kicking a soccer ball is an example of a contact force since two objects, the ball and the foot, are in contact when the force is exerted.
13. D

What Is a Simple Machine?
PS3.D (HIGH SCHOOL)

1. 80%
2. Work is calculated by multiplying the amount of force applied by the distance of motion.
3. A ramp is an example of an inclined plane.
4. Power is the rate at which work is done.
5. The efficiency of a machine may be improved by reducing the

friction produced by the machine and by making the machine more aerodynamic.

6. The SI unit of power is the watt (W). One watt is the amount of power needed to do one joule of work in one second.

7. The mechanical advantage of a machine is defined as the output force divided by the input force, or the input distance divided by the output distance.

8. Simple machines, such as levers, inclined planes, wedges, screws, and wheels and axles, make work easier by changing the force, distance, or direction of the work.

9. A simple machine transfers energy to an object by changing the force, distance, or direction of the work performed on the object.

10. Work is defined as the transfer of energy to an object by the application of a force that causes the object to move in the direction of the force. The amount of work done does not depend on time. Power is the rate at which work is done, or how much work is done in a given amount of time.

11. 180 J
12. 66.7 % efficiency
13. A

What Are Seismic Waves? PS4.A

1. c
2. g
3. e
4. a
5. f
6. b
7. d

8. Seismic waves are mechanical waves that move along Earth's surface (surface waves) or through Earth's interior (body waves).

9. Love waves and Rayleigh waves are the two types of surface seismic waves, and P waves and S waves are the two types of

body seismic waves.

10. All waves, including mechanical waves, carry energy.

11. The fact that S waves cannot move through liquid is important because it allows scientists to make inferences about the states of matter in Earth's interior based on the interaction of body waves, and S waves in particular.

12. Body waves travel more quickly than surface waves, and P waves are the fastest type of body wave, so P waves would be the first type of wave to reach the seismograph.

13. A

What Is Digital Technology? PS4.C

1. Emailing, instant messaging, and social media sites offer greater interconnectedness.

2. Technology is the application of science for practical uses.

3. Today, most systems that use digital technology include a microprocessor, some form of storage, and a software program designed for decision making or information processing.

4. A product that has been completely digitized, such as a movie or song download, is a virtual product.

5. Compressed information takes up less space, can be placed on portable storage modules, and can be easily transported.

6. The Internet is a global system of connected computer networks.

7. Any system is said to be using digital technology if it relies on parts that use binary logic, or a combination of the digits 0 and 1 to represent letters, numbers, characters, and images.

8. A digital system relies on bits to code for letters, numbers, and images.

9. Climate research depends on computers because much of modern climate research is based on complex climate models that

require a great deal of computing power to store and run the programs.

10. Computers are an example of technology. The first computers filled entire rooms. These computers advanced many fields of science by allowing scientists to perform complex calculations more quickly. In turn, scientists developed technology that allowed smaller and faster computers to be built. These computers helped scientists by allowing them to perform even faster calculations and store even more data. So, science and technology rely on each other to grow and advance.

11. Advantages of digital technology include increased communication capabilities, increased access to information, and the ability to download virtual products. Disadvantages of digital technology include identity theft, copyright infringement, and exposure to harmful content. I think the advantages outweigh the disadvantages because of the increased access to information. This sharing of information is important, especially in science.

12. B

How Are Models Used by Scientists and Engineers? ETS1.B

1. A model rocket and a plastic atomic model are examples of physical models.

2. It means that it is repeated until a solution is achieved.

3. Models are used in science to help explain how something works or to describe how something is structured.

4. Mathematical models include sets of equations or computer simulations that generate data that mimic real-world events.

5. Engineering models are used to choose among proposed design

solutions. It is important that the models be accurate so that the best decision can be made.

6. No, physical models can be the same size, or larger, or smaller than the object they are modeling.

7. A model is a representation of an object or a system.

8. Engineers use models to test and evaluate proposed solutions to problems.

9. Engineering and science are two related fields that both use models to enhance their understanding of the objects they are studying.

10. Physical models are physical representations that usually look like the objects they represent. Many physical models are to scale. Conceptual models are used to represent systems of ideas. Conceptual models are often used to relate previously unrelated ideas to one another. Mathematical models use equations, numbers, and data to model a real-world relationship.

11. Scientists and engineers use models in different ways because they are performing different tasks. Scientists are studying the natural world, and models are a tool for understanding and describing what they learn. Engineers are designing structures, machines, and processes that enhance quality of life, and models are used as a tool to help select the best possible solution to a problem.

12. A scientist studying hurricanes would most likely use a mathematical computer model to predict the occurrence of future storms.

13. A

139

CPSIA information can be obtained
at www.ICGtesting.com
Printed in the USA
LVHW011051170921
698050LV00020B/1011